Armies of the Bulgars & Khaɪ Kazan

9th–16th Centuries

Viacheslav Shpakovsky & David Nicolle
Illustrated by Gerry & Sam Embleton
Series editor Martin Windrow

First published in Great Britain in 2013 by Osprey Publishing,
Midland House, West Way, Botley, Oxford, OX2 0PH, UK
43–01 21st Street, Suite 220B, Long Island City, NY 11101, USA
E-mail: info@ospreypublishing.com

OSPREY PUBLISHING IS PART OF THE OSPREY GROUP

© 2013 Osprey Publishing Ltd.

A CIP catalogue record for this book is available from the British Library

Print ISBN: 978 1 78200 079 2
PDF e-book ISBN: 978 1 78200 080 8
ePub e-book ISBN: 978 1 78200 081 5

Editor: Martin Windrow
Index by Zoe Ross
Typeset in Helvetica Neue and ITC New Baskerville
Maps by David Nicolle
Originated by PDQ Media, Bungay, UK
Printed in China through Worldprint Ltd

13 14 15 16 17   10 9 8 7 6 5 4 3 2 1

Osprey Publishing is supporting the Woodland Trust, the UK's leading
woodland conservation charity, by funding the dedication of trees.

www.ospreypublishing.com

Acknowledgements

Our special thanks to N.P. Gordeeva, the guide of Svijajsk, for her kind help
with information and plans; to M.K. Lorents, Departmental Chief of the State
Historical Museum of the Republic of Tatarstan, Kazan, for permitting us to use
several illustrations; and of course to A.S. Sheps, for his excellent line drawings
and for providing map references.

Artist's Note

Readers may care to note that the original paintings from which the colour
plates in this book were prepared are available for private sale. All reproduction
copyright whatsoever is retained by the Publishers. All enquiries should be
addressed to:

www.gerryembleton.com

The Publishers regret that they can enter into no correspondence upon
this matter.

ARMIES OF THE VOLGA BULGARS & KHANATE OF KAZAN 9TH-16TH CENTURIES

INTRODUCTION

From the 7th to the 8th centuries AD, a newly arrived nomadic people appeared in the Middle Volga region of what is now Russia from the south. The name of these Bulgar tribes was first recorded in Byzantine Greek sources. They came from the steppes immediately north of, and around, the Sea of Azov, and their material culture was closely linked to that of the Alans and Sarmatians who also inhabited this territory. However, the Bulgars, unlike those predecessors, belonged to the Turkic linguistic family, suggesting a powerful Turkic influence upon the peoples who had inhabited this region since the time of the Hunnic migrations during the 2nd to 5th centuries AD.

Under pressure from more recently arrived Khazars at the end of the 6th and beginning of the 7th century, the Bulgar tribes separated into two groups. The first moved south-west to the Danube and the Balkan territory of the modern state of Bulgaria, where they were gradually assimilated by the local Slavic population. They soon abandoned their own Turkic tongue to adopt a South Slavic language that evolved into modern Bulgarian; and after a relatively short time, these Balkan Bulgars also adopted the Orthodox Christian faith. Thus was created a substantial state (sometimes known as the First Bulgarian Empire) on the frontiers of the Byzantine Empire.[1]

Meanwhile, the second group of Bulgars migrated north, eventually reaching the basins of the Kama and upper Volga rivers, where forests and fertile valleys had been inhabited by Finno-Ugrian and Turkish tribes since at least the 4th century AD. This second group of Bulgar tribes soon created a 'state' (though that term is not really appropriate for the historical period and social conditions), which was itself under the distant suzerainty of the Khazars. It would remain so for some three centuries, until the Khazar Khanate collapsed in AD 965 after defeat by the Kievan Rus' Prince Sveatoslav.[2]

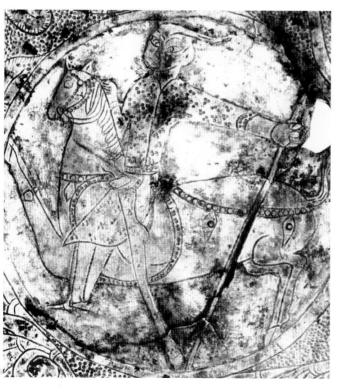

An unarmoured warrior holding a long spear, depicted on a silver bowl made in Volga Bulgar territory and dating from the 10th to 14th centuries. Visible details include the rider's long kaftan-style coat overlapping to the left of the chest, and also the deep, rounded flaps below the saddle – compare with Plate A2. Note also what may perhaps be a bowcase hanging on his left side.

---

1 See Osprey Elite 30, *Attila and the Nomad Hordes*, and ELI 187, *Byzantine Imperial Guardsmen 925–1025*
2 See Men-at-Arms 333, *Armies of Medieval Russia 750–1250*

Apart from the payment of tribute to the Khazar Khanate, the subordination of the Bulgars was not particularly harsh; they were largely left to conduct their affairs independently, as were most other subordinate peoples of the loosely organized but very extensive Khazar Khanate. This was the situation described in AD 922 by the Arab ambassador and Muslim missionary from Baghdad, Ahmad Ibn Fadlan Ibn al-Abbas Ibn Rashid Ibn Hammad (better known to an indebted posterity simply as Ibn-Fadlan), who visited the Volga Bulgars. His primary mission was to convert them to Islam, and to supervise the construction of their first mosque. However, he also kept some sort of journal, and after his return to the Abbasid capital he wrote about his journey to the lands of the *Iltäbär* (vassal ruler) Almish, Yiltawar of the Volga Bulgars. Initially Almish ruled over only one part of this people, but, in line with his efforts to unify them and perhaps even to win independence from the Khazars, he asked for recognition from the Abbasid Caliphate in return for embracing Islam. As part of this process he adopted the Muslim name of Ja'far Ibn 'Abdullah.

This initial conversion was somewhat superficial as far as the majority of his people were concerned, but nevertheless they and their descendants remain Muslim to this day. (The Volga Bulgar state would also endure until, having been defeated by Mongol and Russian armies, its survivors

The Khanate of the Volga Bulgars, 10th–13th centuries, showing the frontiers of c. AD 910.

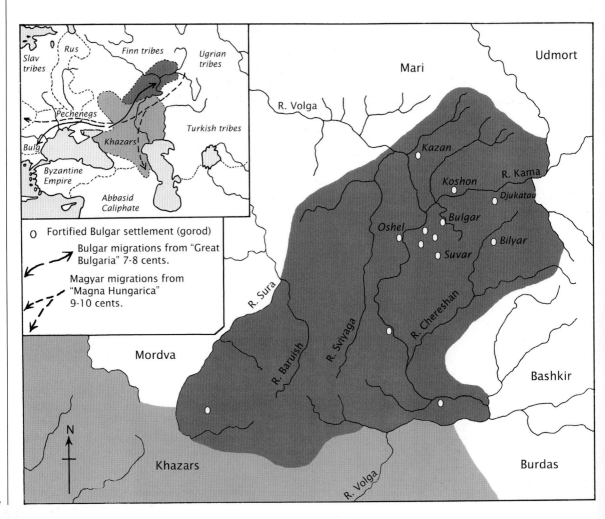

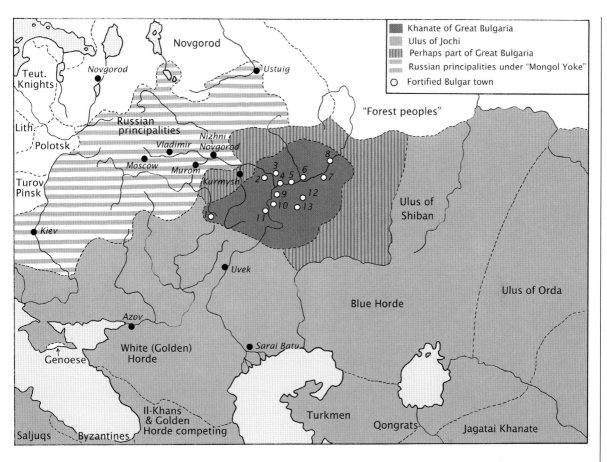

▓	Khanate of Great Bulgaria
▒	Ulus of Jochi
▒	Perhaps part of Great Bulgaria
▬	Russian principalities under "Mongol Yoke"
○	Fortified Bulgar town

Novgorod

Novgorod

Ustuig

Teut. Knights

"Forest peoples"

Lith.

Russian principalities

Polotsk

Nizhni Novgorod

Vladimir

Turov Pinsk

Moscow

Murom

Kurmysh

8

3

5 6

2 4

7

9   12

10 13

11

Ulus of Shiban

Kiev

Uvek

Ulus of Orda

Blue Horde

Azov

White (Golden) Horde

Sarai Batu

Genoese

Il-Khans & Golden Horde competing

Turkmen

Qongrats

Jagatai Khanate

Saljuqs

Byzantines

were assimilated into the post-Mongol Khanate of Kazan – which in many ways could be seen as a continuation of the Volga Bulgar state.)

Once it was unified, the now extensive Islamic khanate along the upper Volga began to play a vital role in long-distance trade between Western Europe, via Scandinavia, the early state of Kievan Rus' (Russia), and the Islamic world to the south. This brought the Volga Bulgars considerable wealth and a variety of cultural connections, and resulted in their acquiring high-quality arms and armour. Most interestingly, this equipment was imported simultaneously from Western Europe, Central Asia to the east, and the Islamic world to the south (though there was also a significant amount of local production).

During the 10th century the Volga Bulgar Khanate developed an export-based economy that grew and flourished, resulting in the building of significant towns with fine public buildings. Surviving remains suggest that the most impressive of these were either religious, such as mosques, or had strong Islamic cultural associations, such as *hamam* public baths. Many of these new towns were also provided with impressive fortifications, mostly of earth and timber but sometimes with stone towers.

Despite a now well-entrenched Islamic identity, after 1100 some Volga Bulgars began to convert to Christianity. This shift in cultural focus (among some, but not all Bulgars) was reflected in certain military equipment, horse-furniture, and even military tactics – a downgrading of traditional Turkish horse-archery in favour of something akin to Western European cavalry close combat.

The Khanate of Great Bulgaria as part of the Mongol *Ulus* Jochi, showing the frontiers of *c*.1270. Town sites: (1) Muksha, (2) Kirman, (3) Kazan, (4) Koshon, (5) Challi, (6) Kurman, (7) Djukatau, (8) Elabugha, (9) Bulgar, (10) Karabulak, (11) Tetush, (12) Bilyar, and (13) Kakresh.

After Mongol generals invaded Russia, and defeated the united forces of the Russian princes and their Kipchak Turkish allies at the bloody battle at Kalka River in 1223, they returned homeward via the territory of the Volga Bulgars.[3] This proved to be a significant error. As the Kurdish-Arab historian 'Ali Ibn al-Athir (1160–1233) wrote in his *Al-Kamil fi al-tarikh* or 'Complete History', when the Bulgars learned of the approach of the Mongols they prepared a great ambush, attacking them from the rear and reportedly killing more than 4,000 of them at the battle of the Samara Bend (September 1223). This significant Mongol reverse, little known outside Russia and a few parts of the Islamic world, was seen as a humiliation that Genghis Khan and his commanders neither forgot nor forgave. The Mongols' revenge was a decade in coming, but it resulted in the devastation of the Bulgars' lands and the burning of their towns in 1236. This Mongol ravaging of Volga Bulgaria went on for five years, and saw the slaughter of what some scholars have estimated to be more than 80 per cent of the population.

Nevertheless, in spite of such utter disasters, the surviving urban population gradually returned to their homes, and the Volga Bulgars regained much of their prosperity by the middle of the 14th century. The town called Bulgar, which had been the capital of their khanate during the 10th and 11th centuries, rose to become a particularly important trade centre during the 13th and 14th centuries, when it was widely known as 'The Great Bulgar'. Meanwhile, the city of Bilyar became the political capital and administrative centre of the khanate. Despite this revival in prosperity, however, the political and military situation of the Volga Bulgars remained difficult.

During the 13th century two significant and previously pagan non-Turkish tribes, the Ves' (or Veps) and the Merya, had been converted to Christianity as a result of increasingly close contacts with the Orthodox Christian principalities of Russia. Like so many of the indigenous peoples in the north-eastern part of European Russia, these Ves' and Merya had spoken languages that were part of the broader Finnish family (they are sometimes called Volga Finns or Eastern Finns, though this identification has been questioned). In the same period other peoples, including the Finno-Ugrian Ugra tribes, had cast off the suzerainty of the Volga Bulgar Khanate; similarly, Bulgar control over the Burtas, Votiaks (Udmurts) and Cheremissians (Mari) was weakening year by year.

The original Volga Bulgar state was destroyed during devastating campaigns by two enemies who were at the same time bitterly hostile to each other: the Russian principalities, and the Mongol Khanate of the Golden Horde (generally referred to as the Tatars). Each feared that the Volga Bulgars would become allies of the other. Thus the Tatar khans burned Bulgar city in 1360, 1362 and 1407, while equally damaging Russian campaigns were waged in 1370, 1374, 1376 and 1409. The final collapse of the Volga Bulgars came in 1431, the year that also saw the emergence of the new town of Kazan – which was initially known as 'New Bulgar'. Within a short period this city became the capital of a new or renamed Khanate of Kazan, which survived until 1552. In that year it finally fell to a Russian army commanded by Grand Prince Ivan IV 'the Terrible' of Moscow, Tsar of all the Russias.

---

3 See Osprey Campaign 98, *Kalka River 1223*

Two riders, one on a mythical winged lion, depicted on a golden ewer forming part of the Nagyszentmiklos Treasure. It was found in Hungary, but may have been of Khazar, Bulgar or early Magyar origin. The horseman wears a long mail hauberk and some type of vambraces; the archer on the winged lion seems to be clad from wrists to knees in 'soft armour'. (Kunsthistorisches Museum, inv. VII.B33, Vienna)

CHRONOLOGY

7th–mid-8th centuries	Bulgar tribes migrate from the Northern Caucasus to the basin of the Svijaga river, a tributary of the Volga.
Mid-9th century	A Bulgar army under the leadership of Khan Adar crosses the Volga and defeats the Magyars, obliging them to migrate to the region between the rivers Don and Dnieper.
922	Embassy from Abbasid Caliphate to Volga Bulgars, led by Ibn-Fadlan; Yiltawar Almish accepts conversion of his realm to Islam.
945	Treaty agreed between Prince Igor of the Kievan Rus' and Emperor Constantine VII of Byzantium to form an alliance against the 'Black Bulgars'.
965	Kievan Rus' army devastates the Khazar capital of Itil' and raids as far as the Islamic frontier; winning access to the Black Sea, they attack the Volga Bulgars to gain control of eastern trade routes.
980	Bulgar campaign against the Rus'.
985	The first Rus' campaign specifically directed against Volga Bulgaria; Rus' Prince Vladimir agrees a treaty of peace between the Rus' and Bulgars that would not be violated for 100 years.
988	Prince Vladimir converts to Orthodox Christianity, obliging the Rus' to do the same.
990	Prince Vladimir of Kiev sends the Byzantine scholar Mark the Macedonian to the Volga Bulgars to spread Christianity; four Bulgar princes convert, and resettle in Kievan territory.
1006	A trade treaty between the Volga Bulgars and the Rus' is mentioned in the chronicles.
1024	Serious famine ('the great hunger') in the Russian Principality of Suzdal'; Russian chronicles state that many Russians travel to Volga Bulgaria to buy bread.
1088	Volga Bulgars attack the town of Murom, capital of a Russian principality of the same name.
1107	Volga Bulgars attack the town of Suzdal', capital of

A model of the late medieval town of Mari, with its typical wooden fortifications. For centuries the Finnish Mari people lived between Volga Bulgar and Russian territory, but they were eventually converted to Orthodox Christianity. (T. Elseev, National Historical Museum of the Mari Autonomous Republic, Yoshkar-Ola; photo V. Shpakovsky)

a Russian principality of the same name.

1120	Russian Prince Jurii Dolgoruky ('Long Arms') attacks the Volga Bulgars, accompanied by the *druzhinas* (princely armies) of Suzdal' and Rostov.
1135, 1145 & 1155	The Arab travellers or geographers Abu Hamid al-Garnati from Andalusia, and Abu Mansur Mawhub al-Jawaliqi from Iraq, visit the Volga Bulgar Khanate and subsequently write descriptions.
1152	Volga Bulgar campaign against Russian Principality of Yaroslavl'.
1164	Prince Andrey Bogolubsky ('the God-Loving') of Vladimir and his brother Yaropolk invade Volga Bulgar territory.
1171	Unsuccessful campaign by Prince Andrey Bogolubsky against Volga Bulgars.
1174	Prince Andrey is assassinated by courtiers conspiring with his second wife, a Volga Bulgar woman seeking revenge for Andrey's persecution of her people.
1183	Rus' attack Volga Bulgars, Kipchaks and Mordvians.
1186	Rus' attack Volga Bulgars.
1209	Volga Bulgars devastate the lands of the Russian Principality of Ryazan.
1218	Russian Principality of Suzdal' attacks the Volga Bulgars.
1217 & 1219	Volga Bulgars seize Unza and Ustug. The armies of the three Russian principalities commanded by the brother of Prince Sveatoslav Vsevolodovich of Novgorod burn the Bulgar town of Oshel'.
1220	Major campaign against Volga Bulgaria by Sveatoslav Vsevolodovich of Novgorod.
1221	Foundation of Nizhniy Novgorod on the site of the destroyed Bulgar town of Oshel'; a six-year armistice is agreed between the Volga Bulgars and Russian principalities.
1223	A substantial Mongol army is ambushed and badly mauled on the Samara river in Volga Bulgar territory.
1229	Mongols attack Volga Bulgars and Kipchaks of the western steppes. Major famine in north-eastern Rus' territory is alleviated when a Bulgar amir sends Prince Yuri Vsevolodovich 30 large river ships loaded with wheat.

1236	A Mongol army destroys Volga Bulgar towns and cities; the territory of Volga Bulgaria is incorporated into the Mongol *ulus* (princely territory) founded by Genghis Khan's eldest son Jochi and currently ruled by his son Batu; nevertheless, Bulgar resistance continues for 40 years thereafter.
1242	The town of Bulgar becomes the capital of Khan Batu's *ulus*.
c.1250–c.1350	The rise of the restored Volga Bulgar Khanate as a part of the wider Mongol Golden Horde.
1276	First mention of the town of Kazan in Russian chronicles, on the occasion when Khan Mengu-Timur gives 'the Bulgarian and Kazan lands' to his son-in-law, Prince Feodor Rostislavich Cherni of Yaroslavl'.
1360	*Ushkuyniki* river-pirates from Novgorod burn the Volga Bulgar town of Jokotin on the Kama river.
1361	Khan Bulak Timur (Tughluq Temur) seizes the city of Bulgar.
1366, 1369, 1370, 1374 & 1375	Repeated raiding by Russian *ushkuyniki* against Volga Bulgar territory of the Khanate of Kazan.
1376	Volga Bulgars pay 3,000 gold *rubles* to the Grand Prince of Russia, plus an additional 2,000 to the Russian *voevodas* (barons) and their warriors, to protect their towns from 'robbery'. Also, first recorded use of firearms by Volga Bulgars against the Russians.
1391–95	The army of Tamerlane (Timur-i Lang) invades Volga Bulgar territory.[4]
1392	Further raids by river-pirates against the towns of Jokotin and Kazan.
1407	Amir Edigei, founder of the Noghay Horde to the south, invades Volga Bulgar territory.
1409	Last mention of *ushkuyniki* river-pirates as a significant threat to the Volga Bulgars.
1431	Prince Vasily II Vasilyevich 'the Blind' of Muscovy sends an army under Prince Feodor Pestry to invade Volga Bulgar territory, crushing the Bulgar forces and devastating the town of Bulgar.
1467–69	Major war between the Russians and the Khanate of Kazan.
1547 & 1550	Two unsuccessful attempts by Grand Prince Ivan 'the Terrible' of Muscovy to conquer Kazan.
1552	Tsar Ivan finally defeats and devastates Kazan, ending the extended history of the old Volga Bulgar Khanate.

Tsar Ivan the Terrible portrayed as St George, defeating Idegäy (Yadigar) Muhammad Ibn Kasim, the last Khan of Kazan, in 1552. This image is from a 17th-century Russian-printed *History of Kazan*.

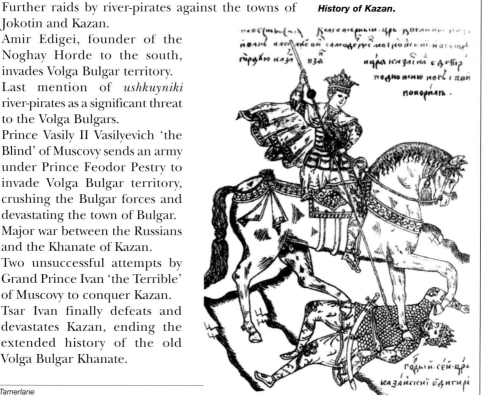

WARS OF THE VOLGA BULGARS

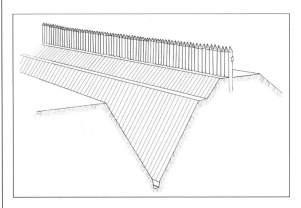

The moat and timber wall of the fortified town of Bulgar in the 10th century. Note the timber facing on the front of the rampart, presumably not only to stabilize the earth but also to make it difficult to climb? The ledge two-thirds of the way up would encourage attackers to pause within easy weapon range of the palisade. (A.S. Sheps, after A. Gubidyllin)

(1) to (4): Daggers of the 10th and 11th centuries.
(5): Volga Bulgar cavalryman's decorated battleaxe.
(A.S. Sheps, after I. Izmailov)

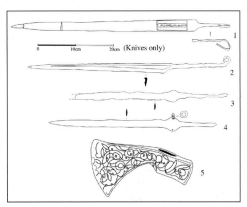

The pre-Islamic period

No unadulterated Volga Bulgar records have survived; most available information comes from contemporary Arabic, Persian, Indian or Russian sources, but archaeological excavations provide useful additional evidence.

It is believed that the territory which became Volga Bulgaria had previously been settled by Finno-Ugrian peoples, including the Mari. Bulgars then moved northwards from the Azov region around AD 660, settling what became their territory during the 8th century, and almost certainly establishing themselves as the dominant population by the close of the 9th century. During this process the Bulgars united various other tribes or peoples of differing origins who lived within this region.

Most scholars agree that the Volga Bulgars were initially subject to the Khazar empire, until the latter's conquest in the later 10th century by Prince Sveatoslav, ruler of the Kievan Rus'. Gradually freed from Khazar domination, this early and still fragmented 'Volga Bulgaria' grew in size, wealth and power. By then an almost entirely unrecorded process of unification was already under way, having started at some time during the late 9th century. The capital of this emerging state was meanwhile established at a location that was called the city of Bulgar, approximately 160km (100 miles) south of the modern city of Kazan. Nevertheless, most scholars doubt that this state of Volga Bulgaria could have truly asserted its independence from the Khazars until the latter were defeated by the Rus' in AD 965.

10th–13th centuries: Islam and its rewards

Islam was adopted as the state religion during the early 10th century as the result of an embassy led by Ibn-Fadlan, who was sent by the Abbasid Caliph al-Muqtadir in AD 922–23. This conversion resulted in the establishment of relations with the distant empire of the Abbasid Caliphate, the despatch of teachers of Islamic law to Volga Bulgaria, and the building of a fortress and a mosque. Subsequently the Volga Bulgars themselves attempted to convert the pagan Rus' Prince Vladimir 'the Great' of Kiev to Islam. According to the chronicler Nestor's account, in AD 987 Vladimir called together exponents of the Jewish, Muslim and Christian faiths. Judaism was rejected for a variety of largely political reasons: it had been the official faith of Kiev's main enemies, the Khazars, and the Jews' ancient loss of Jerusalem was also interpreted as a sign of God's anger towards them. Islam was similarly rejected by Vladimir, because it would have required the Russians to give up wine; the Prince of Kiev reportedly declared that 'Drinking is the joy of all Rus' – we cannot exist without that pleasure'. So Eastern Christianity was selected as the future faith of the Russians, leading to an alliance with the mighty Byzantine Empire.

Prince Vladimir the Great also seized what seemed to be an opportunity to conquer the Volga Bulgars and force them to pay him a tribute. However, according to the chronicles one of his commanders showed Vladimir captives dressed in leather footwear, proclaiming that such people would prove to be bad tributaries, and that it would be wiser to look for people who wore *bast* shoes made of birch-bark. If there is any truth in this story, it probably reflected the fact that the soft-leather boots characteristic of the Bulgars and other Turkic peoples were the mark of horse-riding warriors, whereas footwear made of birch-bark was typical of peasants and farmers.

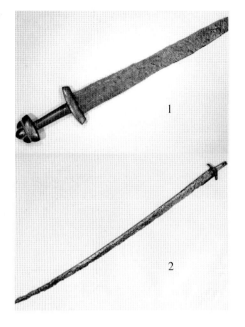

These two weapon finds embody two distinct influences upon the military equipment used in the Volga Bulgar Khanate. (1) Sword, early 11th century; probably of Russian origin, this was found in the territory of the Mordvin – today, Mordovian – people, south-west of the heartland of the khanate. (2) Sabre, 14th century; probably of Turco-Mongol steppe origin, this too comes from Mordvin territory. (Mordovian Republic United Museum of Regional Studies, Saransk, Russian Federation)

The importance of the town of Bulgar (Bulghar, Bolgar) in the 11th century is confirmed by its inclusion – here outlined in a white square, rather vaguely located somewhere north of the Caspian Sea – on a stylized map of the Turks and their neighbours that appeared in the *Diwan Lughat al-Turk* manuscript written by Mahmud al-Kashgari in 1076. (Ms. Ali Emeri, Arabi no. 4189 ff.22–23, Milet Genel Kütüphanesi, Istanbul)

The original Volga Bulgar Khanate thrived as a centre of agriculture as well as handicraft production. By dominating the middle course of the Volga river it controlled much of the trade between Europe, the eastern Islamic world, Central and even Further Asia prior to the Crusades. Its capital of Bulgar developed into a thriving city, rivalling in size and prosperity some great urban centres of the medieval Islamic world. The Volga Bulgars' trading partners included Vikings from Scandinavia, the Yugra (Ugrian) and Nenets peoples of the far north-eastern corner of Europe and north-western Siberia, as well as the great international cities of Baghdad and Constantinople, and merchants were attracted from as far away as Western Europe and China.

Other significant cities or trading towns within the khanate included Bilyar, Suvar (Suwar), Qaşan (Kashan) and Cükätaw (Jokotin), while the modern cities of Kazan and Yelabuga were founded as Volga Bulgar border fortresses. Some other cities mentioned in medieval Russian texts remain unidentified, including Tuxçin (Tukhchin) and İbrahim (Bryakhimov). Most were probably so ruined during the 13th-century Mongol invasion that they were abandoned and forgotten.

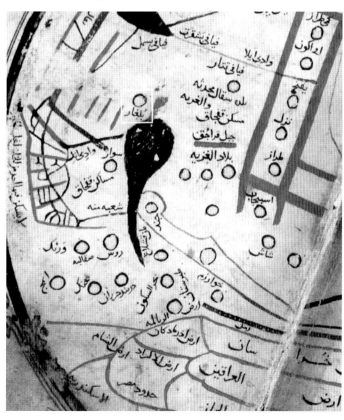

Russian principalities to the west of the Volga Bulgar Khanate posed a significant threat, and during the 11th century the country was devastated by a series of Russian raids. In the late 12th and early 13th centuries the Principality of Vladimir-Suzdal' took the offensive as a means of defending its own eastern borders. Most notable in this regard were Princes Andrey 'the God-Loving' and Vsevolod III, whose armies systematically pillaged Bulgar cities to such a degree that, under this pressure from the west, the Bulgars felt obliged to move their capital from Bulgar to Bilyar.

During the period of their maximum power the Volga Bulgars controlled a substantial territory estimated at around 86,000 square kilometres (33,200 square miles). However, during its first few centuries of existence this Volga Bulgar state remained an island of Islamic territory, cut off from the rest of the early medieval Muslim world by the lands of various pagan or Christian peoples. It was also so far north that several of the daily prayers required of all pious Muslims had to be squeezed into a very short period during the brief daylight hours of a northern winter.

13th century: the coming of the Mongols

In 1223, after defeating an alliance of Russian and Kipchak armies at the battle of the Kalka River, a Mongol army commanded by Subotai and Jebe headed northwards into the territory of the Volga Bulgars. At that point in history Genghis Khan's troops were widely believed to be invincible; nevertheless, to the astonishment of most chroniclers, in late 1223 or 1224 the Bulgars ambushed and defeated Subotai, Jebe and their Mongol army. It would seem that the army led by the Volga Bulgar *Iltäbär* or king Ghabdulla Chelbir fought alongside the armies of two Mordvian tribal *Inäzors* or princes named Puresh and Purgaz. This combined force attacked the Mongol vanguard as they rode alongside a significant bend in the course of the Samara river – hence the clash came to be known as 'the battle of the Samara Bend'. The anti-Mongol Khwarizmi historian al-Nasawi claimed that only 4,000 Mongols survived the battle, but this is unlikely, bearing in mind that the same army under Subotai and Jebe remained strong enough to subdue a Kipchak tribe on its way back to Mongolia. A more restrained account by the Middle Eastern historian Ibn al-Athir merely stated that the Mongols were ambushed in the Volga region, and that after several hard-fought skirmishes with the Bulgars the Mongols tired and moved back down river.

Arrowheads from the Zolotarevskoe fortified settlement, dating from the Mongol siege of 1237. All are Tatar Mongol except for a Russian four-sided crossbow bolt-head – bottom, fourth from left. (State Historical Museum, Penza; photo V. Shpakovsy)

The Koromyslova Tower of the *kremlin* or citadel of Nizhny Novgorod. Founded in 1221 on the site of the Mordvin and Bulgar town of Oshel', burned down in a Novgorod attack, it later passed to Muscovy. The present *kremlin* is one of the oldest brick fortresses in Russia, constructed early in the 16th century as a base from which to attack the Khanate of Kazan. (Photo V. Shpakovsky)

Despite facing a hugely dangerous common foe in the Mongols, the Russian princes persisted in attacking Volga Bulgar territory – presumably because the Bulgars were seen as a traditional rival, whereas the Mongols were as yet an unexpected eruption from a distant quarter, who might never return. The Russian princes also wanted to establish their supremacy in an economically important region to control its considerable sources of revenue. In the event, the Mongols reappeared in 1229 under the command of Kukday and Bubedey, who had been sent with a considerable force by the Great *Khagan* or supreme Mongol ruler, Ogedei. This force defeated what might be described as Bulgar 'frontier guards' at the Ural river and began the occupation of its upper valley in the southern Ural Mountains.

Three years later, in 1232, Mongol cavalry subjugated the south-eastern part of the territory of the Turkic Bashkir people, and occupied southern areas of the Volga Bulgar Khanate itself. However, the Mongols once again failed to capture the Bulgars' main towns and cities. Consequently, at a Great *Kurultai* or gathering in the Mongol capital of Karakorum, it was decided to transfer the best Mongol generals from campaigning in China and the Middle East to lead a major effort to subdue the Volga Bulgar Khanate.

With reportedly more than 300,000 troops, presumably including an effective siege train, Batu Khan struck in 1236. This time the Mongols aimed at the Bulgars' cities; Bilyar, Bulgar, Suvar, Cükätaw, and virtually all the other fortified places fell one after another, their inhabitants being either massacred or sold into slavery. When it was all over, the remains of the Volga Bulgar state became part of the *Ulus* or principality of Genghis Khan's son Jochi, which later became known as the Golden Horde. Bulgar territory was further divided between separate 'duchies' that subsequently emerged as vassals of the Golden Horde, though with some degree of local autonomy.

A bird's-eye view reconstruction of the town of Bulgar as it may have appeared during the 14th century, about a hundred years after its destruction by the Mongols. By this time it had been rebuilt under the new Tatar khans at least to the extent that it was again thought worth raiding by freebooters from Novgorod to the north-west. (A. S. Sheps)

This devastating Mongol conquest effectively destroyed what had been the Volga Bulgar Khanate. The conquerors sacked and ruined all the cities and burned hundreds of towns and villages. According to some historians, more than 80 per cent of the country's population were killed or removed during these years, while those who remained mostly relocated to the northern areas of what had been the old khanate, in what are now the modern territories of Chuvashia and Tatarstan. Subsequently some autonomous duchies re-emerged in these areas, while the steppe regions in the south of the old khanate were settled by nomadic Mongols and Kipchak Turks.

As a result, agricultural development in these latter areas suffered a severe decline. The economy of the Volga Bulgar Khanate is known to have become largely agricultural by the 13th century, the majority of the population consisting of Finno-Ugrian tribes ruled by a Bulgar Turkic elite. Being a settled people, they – unlike the surviving members of the more mobile Bulgar aristocracy – found it much more difficult to migrate elsewhere following the Mongol invasions.

Hence it was largely the remaining settled population who began to rebuild the region's economy, and they succeeded in restoring agriculture outside the steppe regions of what had been the Volga Bulgar Khanate. At the same time the vast and emerging Mongol Golden Horde khanate integrated Volga Bulgar territory into its own economy. Furthermore, it would appear that the Mongols – or 'Tatars', as they came to be known in Russia – learned much from the culture of the old Volga Bulgar state, which became a significant component within broader Tatar-Mongolian culture.

It is important to understand that although the Volga Bulgars had their distinctive traditions prior to the Tatar-Mongolian invasion, the tribes that made up the Volga Bulgar Khanate did not form a single people. Instead the khanate might better be described as a union of tribes or peoples with different languages, and in several cases very different social structures or cultures. After the Mongol invasion the former Bulgar state broke up into several clearly different elements, and even the dominant Turkic part of the former khanate's population no longer referred to themselves as Bulgar; instead they gradually identified themselves with their conquerors, and even called themselves Tatar-Mongols. When the Golden Horde itself fell apart in the 15th century, these people would found a new state called the Tatar Khanate of Kazan. By then the old cities of Volga Bulgaria had been rebuilt, to become significant trade and craft centres within the Golden Horde. Nevertheless, some Bulgar master tradesmen and craftsmen were forcibly moved to Sarai the capital of the Golden Horde, and to other southern cities of that extensive Mongol khanate.

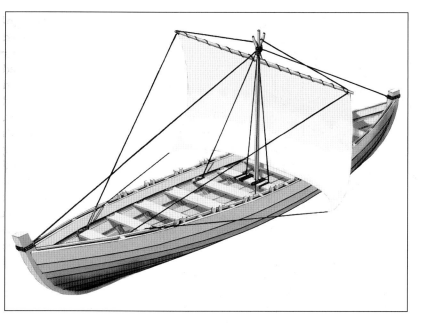

Reconstruction of an *ushkuy* as used by the *ushkuyniki* river-pirates, and probably by many other peoples on the Volga and Kama river system. Clinker-built from pine planks, these craft had a length of 12–14m (39–46ft), a beam of perhaps one-fifth that length, a shallow draught of approximately 0.5m (20in) below the water, and about 1m (39in) of freeboard. This design gave the *uskhuy* considerable speed for a medieval vessel. (A.S. Sheps)

14th century: the scourge of the Novgorod *ushkuyniki*

During the process of the state's re-emergence under its new Tatar khans a new threat erupted from the west, in the form of Russian river-pirates from the Principality of Novgorod. These were the *ushkuyniki*, whose way of life and campaigning recalled the Vikings who had fought, traded and robbed their way along the great rivers of Russia centuries earlier. Their name derives from *ushkuy*, the term for a type of small, shallow-draught Russian ship; the origins of the word are variously identified by scholars.

The *uskhuy* was usually made of pine, the keel being hewn from the trunk of a straight tree. The planking was laid over the vessel's ribs in an overlapping clinker style, recalling the Viking ships of earlier years, the entire structure being held together by wooden pegs. Both on the great rivers and when they ventured into the open sea, the crews could mount amidships a mast or *odnoderevka* ('one timber tree') that carried a single rectangular sail. Yet another feature recalling Viking ships was a seemingly old-fashioned steering-oar, rather than the stern rudder widely adopted by seagoing vessels. The simple steering-oar was less vulnerable to damage in shallow, confined water, and could more easily be raised or removed when the *ushkuy* was portaged overland between rivers – which could be done with ease, by means of rollers. Most historians believe that on the great rivers of Russia an *ushkuy* normally carried about 30 people, or from 4½ to 5 tons of cargo. As far as is known, the river craft used by the Volga Bulgars and their Tatar successors were essentially the same as those of the *ushkuyniki*.

The *ushkuyniki* outlaws would set off from Novgorod along the rivers in search of profit and conquest. They penetrated deeply into the north and into the east of European Russia, and in so doing they greatly extended both the trade and, within a short time, the colonies of the already huge Principality of Novgorod. The most important settlements they founded were along the Northern Dvina, Volga, Kama and Vyatka rivers. The remarkable adventures and achievements of the boldest *ushkuynik* were subsequently immortalized in the epic '*Vasily Buslaev*'.

The *ushkuyniki* were professional fighters, capable of facing both infantry and cavalry. Generally speaking, they had good military equipment; evidence shows that many possessed Western-style mail hauberks, though it was probably more common for them to wear various hybrid assemblages of armour purchased or looted from a variety of sources. Thus one man might wear elements of mail, lamellar or scale armour at the same time; the composite mail-and-plate (or more accurately, mail-and-laminated) *bechterets* was particularly popular. This armour, perhaps of ultimately Persian origin, would become typical of later medieval and early modern Russia, providing considerable flexibility and freedom of movement

The Northern Mausoleum in the ruins of the fortified medieval city of Bulgar; built in the mid-14th century, it overlooks the Volga river. This structure now houses a collection of Islamic tombstones from the territory of the Volga Bulgar state; the rectangular modern roof protects the masonry from the severe weather characteristic of this region. (Photo V. Shpakovsky)

while also covering the wearer's chest and back with small, overlapping laminated steel plates. Such first-class gear was, of course, owned by *ushkuyniki* leaders and those in the front ranks of combat, while other men had to make do with inferior equipment.

Their weaponry was similarly influenced by their Mongol-Tatar foes consisting for close combat of the usual array of spears, swords and sabres – the latter clearly being preferred. Longer-range weapons included bows and crossbows; the *ushkuynikis'* crossbows were particularly feared by the Volga Bulgar and Kazan Khanate troops for their accuracy, range and armour-piercing bolts. Very often such superior military equipment and the money needed to mount ambitious expeditions, were given to the *ushkuyniki* by rich *boyars* (noblemen) or merchants of Novgorod who saw such forays as commercial investments. In this they were often proved correct, being handsomely compensated by returning *ushkuynik* with shares of their loot.

In 1366, three noblemen of Novgorod – Osip Warphalomeevich, Vasily Pfedorovich and Alexander Abakumovich – seized the merchant caravans travelling between Nizhniy Novgorod and Kazan. Because the available army of the Mongol Horde was weaker than that of the *ushkuyniki* who carried out this attack, the Khan of Kazan asked his vassal Dmitrii Ivanovich the Prince of Moscow, for help. Dmitrii, who would later be known as 'Donskoy' because of his victory over a Tatar army near the Don river sent a threatening letter to the rulers of Novgorod, insisting that they make good the damage done. However, the *boyars* replied that the attack had been helpful to the Rus', while another letter maintained that 'The young men [referring to the *ushkuyniki*] travelled to the Volga river without our permission'. Furthermore, they had not robbed 'guests' or travellers, but had only hurt Muslims. In reality, of course, the *ushkuynik* were operating with the full knowledge and approval of Novgorod's leaders, amongst whom aggression against Muslims was considered to be entirely legitimate behaviour.

Between 1360 and 1375 the *ushkuyniki* are known to have undertaken eight major campaigns plus countless smaller operations in the middle Volga region alone, and their frequent victories over the Tatars were proudly recorded by Novgorod's chroniclers. In 1369, ten *ushkuy* vessels travelled along the Volga and Kama rivers before joining forces inside Volga Bulgar territory. In the following years they cruised the Volga twice, and made several brutal assaults upon the local population. They by no means limited their depredations to Muslim territory, however; in 1369 and 1370 more *ushkuyniki* seized control of the Christian Russian towns of Kostroma and Yaroslavl'.

In 1374 a force of some 2,700 from Novgorod sailed downstream from the headwaters of the Volga to rob Vyatka. They then managed to seize the city of Bulgar itself, and, having robbed its people, they threatened to burn it to the ground; in desperation the citizens paid them 300 *rubles*, which was then a considerable sum. Once they had extracted this protection money the *ushkuyniki* split into two detachments. One group, with 50 ships, sailed on down the Volga as far as the Golden Horde's capital of Sarai. A second detachment 1,200 strong sailed up the Volga, devastating Chuvash and Mari settlements.

The fiercest raid by Novgorod's *ushkuyniki* took place in 1375, when (according to the Russian historian N. Kostomarov) a detachment of 1,500–2,000 aboard no fewer than 70 *ushkuy* appeared near Kostroma, a town belonging to the Prince of Moscow. Around 5,000 armed citizens assembled on the shore, and when they saw this gathering the *ushkuyniki* began to separate into groups. One party advanced against those on the shore, while another went around to their rear into the forest or dense thickets of junipers. When they launched their two-pronged attack on the townspeople the defenders' commander, named Plesheev, was apparently the first to flee, abandoning his compatriots and running back to Kostroma, whereupon the rest followed suit. The Novgorod *ushkuyniki* killed some of those who were fleeing, and seized and bound others, though the remainder had time to hide in the forest. When the pirates reached the now defenceless town they looted it thoroughly, then settled down there for a while.

Having rested for a couple of weeks in Kostroma, the *ushkuyniki* sailed on down the Volga to Bulgar and Sarai, which had already been 'visited' and looted by previous river-pirates. All that the rulers of Bulgar could do was offer the Novgorod *ushkuyniki* a substantial bribe, to add to the

The Small Minaret in Bulgar city was built between 1340 and 1400, traditionally on the site of the 'Saints of the Bulgars'. It stands next to the so-called Khan's Tomb, which also dates from the 14th century. (Photo V. Shpakovsky)

loot and the women who had been seized in Kostroma. Moving on to Sarai, the pirates took the Golden Horde Khan's capital by storm, and again seized everything valuable they could carry. This time, despite a near-anarchy that was threatening to tear the Golden Horde apart, the local ruler Khan Salgey invited his unwelcome 'guests' to a feast. According to the sources, the men of Novgorod began to 'drink until they appeared to be dead drunk', giving the Muslim defenders a chance to capture the *ushkuyniki* camp and exterminate the invaders in the greatest defeat they ever suffered. Nevertheless, this episode emphasized the strength rather than the weakness of the river-pirates: the Tatars had not even tried to defeat them in open battle (or when they were sober).

In 1391 and 1392, pirates joined with the people of Ustug to campaign along the Vyatka, Kama and Volga rivers, robbing travellers and capturing the towns of Jokotin and Kazan in successive years. In 1409 there was yet another raid into Volga Bulgaria by large numbers of ships moving along the Kama and Volga, but this time the pirates undermined their campaign by dividing their strength. A force heading along the Kama was attacked and defeated by the Tatars, while the ships moving along the Volga failed to come to their aid. Thereafter information about the *ushkuyniki* disappears from the record. Seemingly they were not only banished but, according to the modern Russian historian A. Shirokorad, the later 15th- and 16th-century rulers of Muscovy imposed strict censorship of historical chronicles (presumably to draw a veil over a story that might prove dangerously inspiring to future adventurers).

The Khanate of Kazan, showing the frontiers of c.1500.

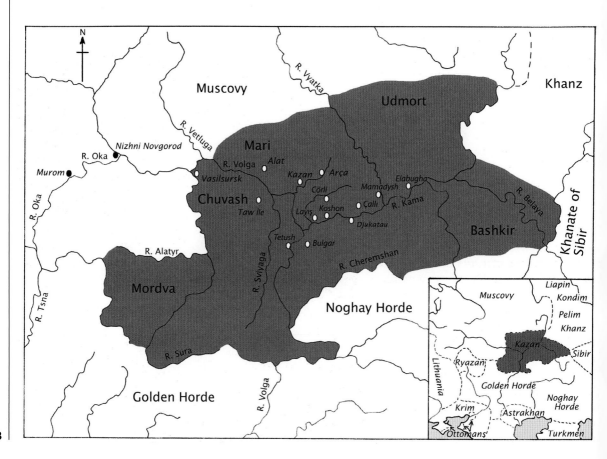

15th century: the Khanate of Kazan

The first written evidence of the existence of the city of Kazan dates from 1391, when it was described in the *Rogozhsky Chronicle* as the centre of a Bulgar 'sultanate'.

According to some sources, a generation or so later in either 1437 or 1438, Kazan was conquered by Oluğ Muhammad, the deposed Khan of the Golden Horde, who thereby established the Khanate of Kazan as a separate political entity. According to other scholars, it was Oluğ Muhammad's son Mahmud who seized Kazan in 1445 and made it the new state's capital. Whatever the truth, Oluğ Muhammad used his new realm as a launch-pad for a series of raids against the Russian Principality of Moscow (Muscovy). The first of these reportedly took place in 1439, and thereafter Oluğ's raids penetrated deep into Russian territory. In the spring of 1445 Grand Prince Vasily II of Moscow was even captured by the Kazan Tatars; his people were forced to pay a large ransom for their ruler's release, and Muscovy was also obliged to sign a treaty beneficial to Kazan.

Grand Prince Ivan III 'the Great' of Muscovy (1462–1505) formed an alliance with Khan Kasim of Kasimov, another of Oluğ Muhammad's sons, who ruled a small khanate south-east of Moscow. When Ivan III agreed to help Kasim win the throne of Kazan this sparked a hard-fought Russo-Kazan War in 1467–69. In September 1469, after many setbacks, Russian troops were finally able to besiege Kazan itself and, by cutting the city's access to water, forced its people to sue for peace. A new treaty was concluded, this time beneficial to the Russians, and large numbers of Russian prisoners were released. Kasim Ibn Oluğ Muhammad nevertheless failed to become Khan of Kazan, and was in fact even replaced as Khan of Kasimov by his son Daniyar.

A reconstruction by F.K. Valeev of part of the *kremlin* or citadel of Kazan, as it appeared on the eve of the Russian conquest in the mid-16th century. (ex-Valeev & Valeeva-Suleimanova, *Drevnee Iskusstvo Tatarstana* – see below, 'Further Reading')

The Khanate of Kasimov has been described as 'a historical curiosity', being based around the previously Russian town of Gorodets on the Oka river, which had been given by Prince Vasily I of Muscovy to Kasim when the latter sought refuge in Moscow. It was then renamed after the refugee khan, whose successors were, paradoxically, often referred to as *tsars*, despite their being feudal vassals of the Grand Princes – later Tsars – of Moscow. Some of the later Khans of Kasimov converted to Christianity and entered Russian service, their little state eventually being annexed by Russia in 1681.

The last 40 years of the existence of the Khanate of Kazan coincided with the expansion of Moscow's power over Russia and the fading of Tatar power. Within Kazan itself this period was characterized by a bewildering series of conspiracies, disputed successions and dethronements, during which

various rulers of this chronically unstable and disunited kingdom were nevertheless still able to defy Muscovy on a number of occasions.

The death in 1479 of Khan Ibrahim of Kazan was followed by a power struggle that resulted in his son Ilham (also known as 'Ali Ibn Ibrahim) winning the throne. However, the new khan's brother Muhammad Amin, like Kasim before him, decided to flee to Moscow to serve Grand Prince Ivan III. In 1484 Ilham was deposed by the pro-Muscovite faction in the khanate, being replaced with the still young Muhammad Amin. He in turn failed to retain the throne, being deposed the following year when Ilham returned. Angered by the fall of his preferred candidate, Ivan III launched yet another campaign again Kazan in 1487. The Russians again managed to take control of the city, captured Ilham, and again replaced him with Muhammad Amin. From this time onwards Grand Prince Ivan III used the style of 'Duke of Bulgaria' amongst his numerous other titles.

The strong Muscovite influence over Khan Muhammad Amin led in 1495 to another factional attempt to replace him, this time with Mamuq Ibn Ibaq, Khan of the Siberian Tatars (Sibir). Mamuq himself proved so unpopular that he too had to flee; but rather than having Muhammad Amin back, the nobles of Kazan asked Grand Prince Ivan III to send them Muhammad's brother Abd al-Latif Ibn Ibrahim (Ğäbdellatíf) instead. When they got him, the Tatar nobles soon changed their minds yet again, and – perhaps reluctantly – asked Ivan III to again re-establish Muhammad Amin as khan, this being his third reign.

Russian *streltsy* infantry armed with hand-held guns attacking Kazan, as shown in a 16th-century Russian woodcut print.

16th century: resistance to Muscovy, and fall

In 1505, in anticipation of the aged Grand Prince Ivan III's death, Muhammad Amin decided to assert his independence of Muscovy. This he did in dramatic fashion, by massacring many Russians living within the Khanate of Kazan; he then invaded Russian territory, taking his former allies completely by surprise. After Ivan's death in October 1505 the new Grand Prince Vasily III sent an army against Kazan, but this suffered a crushing defeat at the battle of Arsk Field in 1506. Nevertheless, Muhammad Amin thought it best to sue for peace, and paid homage to Vasily.

Twelve years later he himself died without a male heir. In this crisis the 11-year-old Shah ‘Ali Ibn Sayyid (Şahğäli), Khan of Kasimov, was offered the crown of Kazan. Regarded as an unpopular puppet of Muscovy, in 1521 Khan Shah ‘Ali was deposed by nobles who formed a conspiracy with Sahib Giray, brother of Khan Muhammad (Mehmed) I Giray of the Khanate of Krim (Crimea). The latter was deeply hostile to Russia, and maintained increasingly close relations with the Ottoman Sultans. Russians living within the territory of the Khanate of Kazan were once again slaughtered. Later in 1521 a combined army from the khanates of Kazan and Crimea launched a devastating raid deep into Russian territory, concluding with a siege of Moscow itself, after which the Grand Prince of Muscovy was obliged to pay tribute to the Crimean Tatars.

Stone cannon-balls used by Russian gunners during the 1552 siege of Kazan. Grand Prince Ivan IV ‘the Terrible’ invested heavily in his artillery train, and massive bombards were cast for siege work. Six years after the fall of Kazan, the English ambassador Fletcher would write of the palace armoury in the Moscow *kremlin* that ‘No one sovereign in Christendom has so many guns as them... all cast from bronze and extremely beautiful’. (State Historical Museum of Tatarstan, Kazan; photo V. Shpakovsky)

In 1524 the Russians retaliated by sending an army against Kazan led by Prince Ivan Belsky, whose siege of Kazan forced the city to ask for terms. Prince Ivan, whose army was running out of provisions, felt that he had no choice but to agree, but his decision was nevertheless regarded in Moscow as treasonable. Meanwhile, Khan Sahib Giray of Kazan was more interested in affairs in the Crimea and so returned home, leaving Kazan in the hands of his 14-year-old nephew Safa Giray.

Grand Prince Vasily's final war against Kazan started in the spring of 1530. Although the defences had been reinforced during the previous years of peace, Russian troops soon besieged Kazan itself, and Khan Safa Giray fled in 1531. For a variety of reasons Russian commanders then missed their chance to seize the virtually deserted city before Kazan troops returned to the field. The Tatars launched a damaging attack upon the Russian army, forcing it to abandon the siege and enter peace talks.

By then yet another conspiracy had been hatched by a group of Kazan nobles, to depose Khan Safa Giray and request of Moscow that Canğäli, a brother of Shah ‘Ali Ibn Sayyid (Şahğäli), be nominated as their ruler in his place. Canğäli arrived in 1530/31 to rule the khanate under the domination of his Muscovite protectors. However, these events were merely a prelude to the campaigns of Grand Prince Ivan IV ‘the Terrible’ of Moscow and Russia against the Khanate of Kazan in 1547 and 1550, and its final devastation in 1552.[5] This resulted in the Russian occupation of the entire territory of what had once been the extensive Volga Bulgar Khanate, and in Ivan the Terrible adding the title of *Tzar' Bolgarsky* (Emperor of the Bulgars) to the already lengthy ‘throne titles’ of the Russian tsars – a title which the Romanovs would retain until 1917.

5   See MAA 427, *Armies of Ivan the Terrible*

ARMIES: ORGANIZATION & TACTICS

During the earliest period of Volga Bulgar history their military organization was based upon essentially the same principles as the medieval Russian *druzhina*, the armed following of a ruler or leading aristocrat. Thus Volga Bulgar rulers built their military forces and pursued their policies using their own *druzhinas*; these consisted of *hashum*, which in modern terms might be called 'guards', supported by a secondary force called the *hyane*, which was in effect the 'youngest *druzhina*'. The leaders of the *hashum* and the local nobility had real power in their hands, and provided the foundation of the Volga Bulgars' entire military system from the 10th to the 13th centuries. The earliest written sources, dating from the 9th and 11th centuries, confirm that the Volga Bulgars had two significant towns each of which could supposedly field 10,000 horsemen, whereas the khan's *druzhina* numbered only 500 fighting men. By the 12th and 13th centuries it is clear that the population of the Volga Bulgar Khanate had increased significantly, and with it the size of the state's army. Some chronicles even claimed that in 1172 the Bulgar detachment that repulsed Russian invaders consisted of between 6,000 and 7,000 warriors, while in one of their battles the Bulgars reportedly lost between 1,000 and 3,500 men, this number representing only part of their overall force.

In the 10th and 11th centuries the number of *yori* (a term that might be interpreted as 'knights' fiefdoms') in the khanate amounted to holdings held by up to 10 per cent of the male population. In most parts of Western Europe those who held comparable knightly estates were normally around 2 per cent of the population. Thus, based upon the most recent population estimates for the Volga Bulgar Khanate, we might calculate that there were between 15,000 and 20,000 mounted warriors. On the other hand, the steeply rising cost of cavalry equipment, including arms and armour, led this proportion to fall during the 12th and 13th centuries to between 3 and 5 per cent, thus say 7,000–10,000 cavalry. The rising cost of a warrior's equipment was

The military organization of the Volga Bulgar state during the 10th and 11th centuries. (A.S. Sheps)

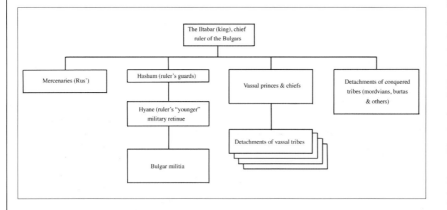

The military organization of the Volga Bulgar state during the 12th and 13th centuries. (A.S. Sheps)

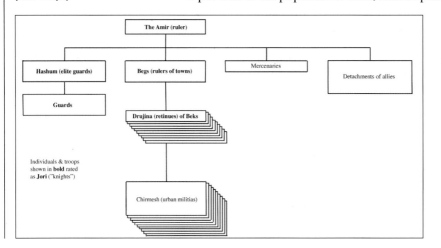

largely the result of a gradual change from an essentially Turkish 'steppe' style of cavalry warfare to a more European style of close cavalry combat.

Of course, the subordinated chiefs of the Mari, Mordvians and other tribes also contributed warriors to the army of Volga Bulgaria. It is in this context that one visiting Arab traveller mentioned the term *saria* to describe the detachment of one such tribal prince, which consisted of 4,000 horsemen.

Volga Bulgar tactics were initially the same as those common to all steppe nomads. According to eyewitnesses, in battle they normally adopted a formation consisting of ranks, in which the archers moved around harassing the enemy while Bulgar light and heavy cavalry either charged directly forwards or tried to attack the enemy's flanks. These were essentially the same tactics as used by Seljuk Turks, Kipchaks, and Magyars or early Hungarians. At the centre of a Volga Bulgar army would be the commander's banner, while signals would be given by means of trumpeters.

ARMS & ARMOUR

Swords and sabres

Amongst the most interesting archaeological finds of early medieval military equipment within what was once the territory of the Volga Bulgars were no less than 12 Carolingian–style swords plus their fragmentary hilts. These were probably made in the Rhineland area of Germany, and it may be that Volga Bulgar territory represented the most easterly limit of normal distribution for such weapons; potential other examples found even further afield are likely to have been combat trophies or even totemic objects. Those from Volga Bulgaria, however, may simply have been purchases, via arms traders, almost directly from their place of manufacture. The typical Carolingian sword was quite a heavy weapon, with a straight double-edged blade and a massive hilt of distinctive form.

Three of those found in this context even had that most characteristic of early medieval blade inscriptions - the word ULFBERHT in large Latin letters. This is well known to European historians as a sort of 'trademark' for a highly respected centre of sword–making, if not necessarily for a single workshop. Its products have been found across most of Europe from the end of the 9th into the early 11th centuries, though more particularly in northern and eastern regions. The manufacturing centre itself is believed to have been located on the middle Rhine, between the towns of Mainz and Bonn.

Two such swords with inscriptions, currently displayed in the State Historical Museum of the Republic of Tatarstan at Kazan, are particularly well preserved. Based upon the design of their hilts they have been identified as Types S and probably T-2, according to the widely-used classification system devised by the Norwegian scholar J. Petersen. The first example, Type S, dates back to the second half of the 10th or first half of the 11th century. It has a massive pommel divided into three parts, rounded at the top and the ends, all these elements being attached to a foundation by rivets.

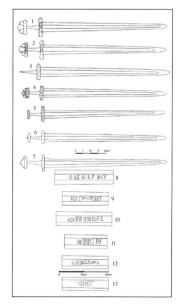

(1) to (7): 10th–11th-century swords imported from Western or Central Europe, found in Volga Bulgar territory. (8) to (13): Enlarged details of inscriptions and decoration on European-style blades from Volga Bulgar territory. (A.S. Sheps, after I. Izmailov)

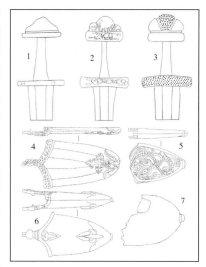

(1) to (3): Sword hilts from Volga Bulgar territory, 10th–11th centuries.
(4) to (7): Scabbard chapes from Volga Bulgar territory, 10th–12th centuries.
(A.S. Sheps, after I. Izmailov)

(1) to (9): Spear and javelin heads from Volga Bulgar territory, 10th–11th centuries.
(10) to (17): Heavy cavalry spearheads, 11th–13th centuries.
(A.S. Sheps, after I. Izmailov)

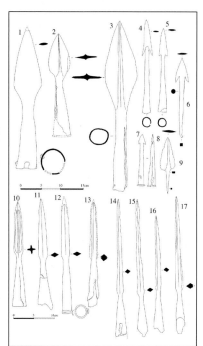

In the opinion of the Russian medieval weapons specialist A. Kirpichnikov, the second of these swords is an example of the rarer Type T-2, and should be dated to the 10th century. Its guard or cross-piece has decorations consisting of three horizontal lines of large 'cells', which are connected to each other by narrow diagonal channels cut out of the guard and filled with twisted silver wire. The ends of these bands of decoration are formed by such wire being rolled into loops, while in the centre the two rows of silver wire form crosses. Unfortunately the pommel is missing, but it was almost certainly decorated in the same manner.

Another sword had the blade inscription LEUTFRIT or LEUTLRIT, which has again been found in other parts of Europe, from Estonia to the British Isles. On the other side of the blade was an apparent 'running animal', probably a very early version of the well-known 'wolf' stamp that came into use during the 13th century and which is widely associated with the German blade-making centre of Solingen.

Unfortunately, these swords from the territory of the Volga Bulgars were chance finds rather than the results of archaeological excavation, so their precise find locations and contexts are unknown. It cannot be stated with certainty whether they belonged to Bulgar warriors or to merchants or mercenaries from other places. What is clear is that such magnificent weapons must have been expensive; they would surely have belonged only to men of considerable wealth, or have been a gift or reward from a ruler.

Because Volga Bulgar cavalry had to face not only the heavily armoured warriors of Russian *druzhinas* but also steppe nomads, they usually used relatively light, curved sabres rather than heavy, straight swords; the former enabled them to make more rapid fencing movements while on horseback. The sabre developed amongst the nomadic peoples of the Eurasian steppes, probably during the 7th or 8th century AD, and early forms had been well known among the Bulgars since at least the period of the Khazar Khanate.

Most of the sabres found in this region are highly corroded, but two are in a much better state of preservation. One such blade, actually found within the area of Bulgar town itself, has a long and narrow blade that tapers smoothly towards the point. The steel crossguards of these weapons often had down-sloping quillons with ball or diamond-shaped terminals and flattened sides, which provided good protection to the user's hand. Scabbards for these Volga Bulgar sabres were made of wood, with a leather covering and often decorated bronze chapes, lockets, and mounts for straps to a sword-belt. Following the Mongol invasions the sabre became an even more typical weapon of the cavalry of the Khanate of Kazan, remaining so until its final fall in the 16th century.

Spears and javelins

Amongst the Volga Bulgars, as among other Eurasian peoples, spears saw very widespread use. These ranged from simple thrust weapons for use on foot and on horseback, to more specifically armour-piercing forms that would probably have been used by elite Bulgar cavalry. The simpler spears with leaf-shaped blades were used by ordinary infantry. Javelins of a type known among the Russians as a *sulitisa* were also mentioned, apparently being used by both infantry and cavalry to oppose Tatar archery.

(continued on page 33)

BULGARS & SUBJECTS, 9th–10th CENTURIES
1: Bulgar leader, 10th century
2: Bulgar cavalryman, 9th–10th centuries
3: Infantry archer of subject tribe, 10th century

A

BULGARS & ALLIES, 11th–12th CENTURIES
1: Bulgar cavalryman, 11th–12th centuries
2: Khanty tribal warrior, 11th–12th centuries
3: Mari tribal warrior, 11th century

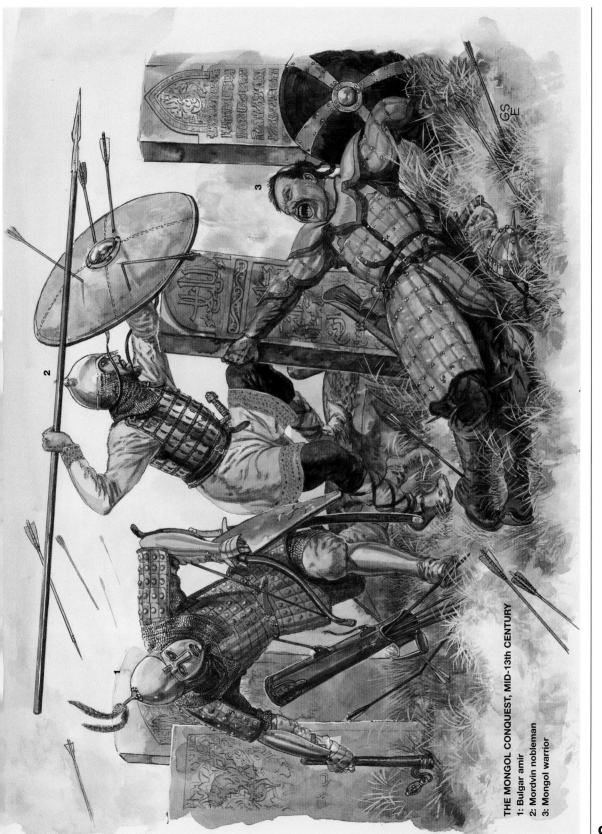

THE MONGOL CONQUEST, MID-13th CENTURY
1: Bulgar amir
2: Mordvin nobleman
3: Mongol warrior

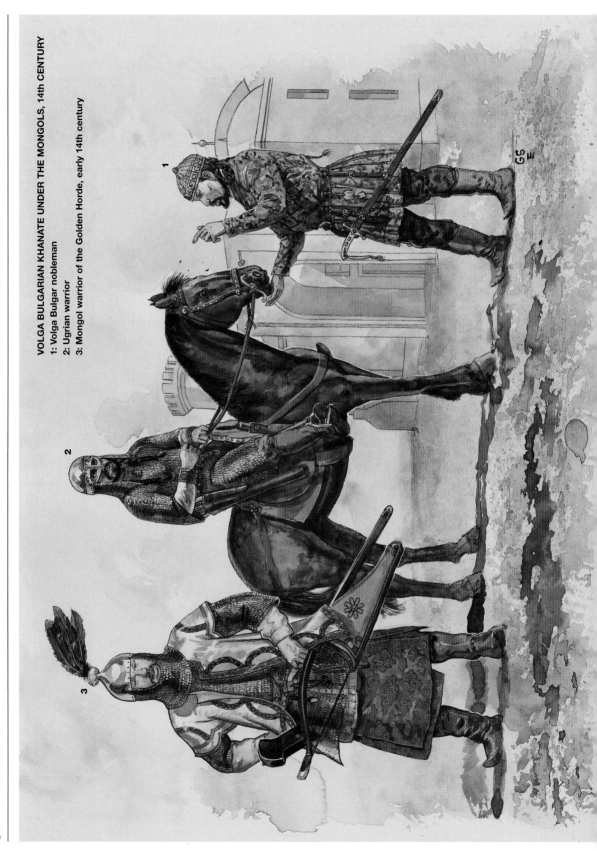

VOLGA BULGARIAN KHANATE UNDER THE MONGOLS, 14th CENTURY

1: Volga Bulgar nobleman
2: Ugrian warrior
3: Mongol warrior of the Golden Horde, early 14th century

D

THE *USHKUYNIKI* MENACE, 14th–15th CENTURIES
1: High-status Bulgar warrior; 14–15th centuries
2: Archer; 14–15th centuries
3: Siberian mercenary; 14th century

E

KHANATE OF KAZAN, 15th–EARLY 16th CENTURIES
1: Khan, early 16th century
2: Palace guardsman, late 15th century
3: Siberian tribal ally, 15th–16th centuries

KHANATE OF KAZAN INFANTRY, 15th–EARLY 16th CENTURIES

1: Hand-gunner, early 16th century
2: Infantry archer, late 15th century
3: Fully armoured soldier, late 15th century

THE FALL OF KAZAN, 1552
1: Dismounted officer
2: Noghay warrior
3: Allied officer, Khanate of Sibir

H

Battleaxes

The most commonly found weapon was the axe, which came in a variety of forms. Battleaxes were often decorated, but simple axes of working form were commonly used as weapons by the peasant militias. Some of the most distinctive axes found in the territory of the Volga Bulgars had an additional, sharply curved beak or hammerhead on the back; these weapons were known as *chekans* in Russia. Some small battleaxes were decorated with a damascened surface having gold and silver wire hammered into engraved grooves, and during the 9th to 10th centuries axes of the *chekan* type were almost certainly used as signs of rank as well as serving as functional weapons. From the 10th to 13th centuries their military use seemingly changed, coinciding with the appearance of some newer types. The light, armour-breaking or armour-piercing axe that had become the most typical weapon of an elite Volga Bulgar cavalryman evolved into the almost universal pole-axe so widely used by foot-soldiers.

Maces and bludgeons

Maces and bludgeons were among the traditional weapons used by the Volga Bulgars, especially when facing Russian warriors. Their construction was generally simple, consisting of a metal head pierced by a hole for the attachment of a haft. The earliest examples of this weapon were actually found in the territory of the Khazar Khanate, but no fewer than 17 various types of metal mace have so far been found within the territory of the Volga Bulgars. They include the 'winged mace' or *shestoper*, used by the Volga Bulgars as well as several peoples in the Islamic Middle East since at least the 13th century, and adopted by Western European knightly cavalry during the 14th century. The well-known Russian historian of weaponry, A. Kirpichnikov, maintains that the Volga Bulgars' use of winged or flanged *shestopers* proves that this weapon was widely seen in Eastern Europe during that period.

One of the maces found in Volga Bulgaria has a beak-like knob and is round in section. When used with accuracy and skill, the point of this mace made it an effective armour-breaking weapon. Another interesting mace found in a Volga Bulgar site has four large central knobs in the form of small pyramids, plus eight smaller knobs on its sides. This design meant that whichever part of the mace struck a target, one of these pointed pyramids would concentrate the weight of the weapon and the force of the blow. The construction of such maces is also distinctive, their complex shapes and their external appearance being the result of casting in clay moulds while leaving an empty space inside. This would be filled with lead, producing a heavier and potentially devastating weapon.

Because the mace was used as a mark of social status, the weapons themselves varied. There were highly decorated and structurally complicated examples, which were almost certainly associated with professional *drujinniks* or members of an aristocratic military retinue. Others might be described as simple 'democratic' variants used by low-ranking soldiers recruited from towns and villages. Here it is worth noting that the Volga Bulgar name for a mace in pre-Mongol times was *kurzi* (*gurz* in Turkish and Persian), as confirmed in literary sources.

The State Historical Museum of the Republic of Tatarstan has the heads of several interesting bludgeons or war-flails on display. In fact no

11th-century spearheads from the south-western part of the khanate; (2) is classified as a cavalry weapon. (Mordovian Republic United Museum of Regional Studies, Saransk, Russian Federation)

(1) Bronze axe-head, Volga Bulgar, 10th–11th centuries (ex.I. Ismailov); (2) bronze axe-head, 10th–12th centuries. (ex-Valeev & Valeeva-Suleimanova)

(1) & (2): Battleaxes, 9th–11th centuries; (3) axe with 'hammer' head, probably for a cavalryman, 9th–11th centuries. (Mordovian Republic United Museum of Regional Studies, Saransk, Russian Federation)

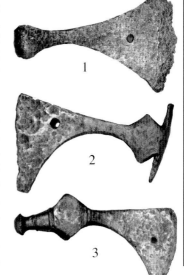

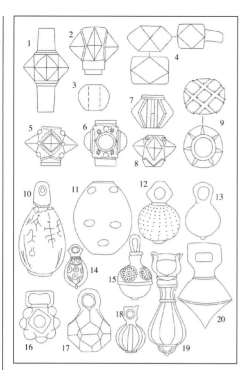

(1) to (9): Selection of simple, flanged and knobbed Bulgar mace-heads dating from the 10th to 13th centuries. (10) to (20): Various types of 'weights' or striking-heads from Volga Bulgar war-flails or bludgeons, made to be attached to a cord or strap rather than directly to a haft. (A.S. Sheps, after I. Izmailov)

fewer than 33 such weapons have been found within the autonomous territory of Tatarstan, surely indicating that its use was widespread. It normally consisted of one or more metallic heads attached by a strap or cord to a short haft (the strap might also have been simply held in the hand, but the extension of the head's arc of swing would make a hafted weapon more powerful). Some of the warheads from such weapons are of metal, usually bronze, but others are made of bone. In the latter case the striking-heads are egg-shaped, highly polished, and with various engraved motifs. In some cases the bronze or bone heads were hollow inside and filled with lead, to make them considerably heavier. In other cases their surfaces had hollows which were then filled with lead, as seen in an example from the town of Bilyar (see image 11 in the accompanying panel of drawings). Archaeologists believe that most of these strange weapons date from the 10th to 12th centuries. A well-made, pear-shaped bronze striking-head with a large eye and two flanges was also found in the town of Bulgar, though this is thought to date from the 13th or 14th century.

Perhaps these weapons indicate that armour and particularly helmets were relatively uncommon amongst the majority of poorer warriors, since such war-flails would not have been very effective against a heavily protected opponent. It is nevertheless interesting to recall their use in the late 12th- or early 13th-century German *Nibelungenlied* ('Song of the Nibelungs'), during a combat between the dwarf Alberich and the hero Siegfried. By placing this 'scourge' in the hands of the wicked dwarf the author indicated that, for the Germans, the war-flail was seen as an alien weapon:

The scourge with seven knobs,
So heavy, the fierce Alberich with its help
Broke the hero's shield in parts
With one well-aimed blow.

Bows and arrows

The most important long-range weapon used throughout Eastern Europe, including the territory of the Volga Bulgars, was the bow. Even today a remarkable variety of arrowheads continue to be uncovered across the entire territories of the modern Republic of Tatarstan and of the preceding Khanate of the Volga Bulgars. The bow typically used from the time of the earliest Bulgar incursion was the recurved type, constructed either of laminated wood or of a composite of wood, bone and sinew, which gave great power for its length. The bow featured prominently in tales of the *amir* or Khan Idegäy (Edigei), hero of the Tatar folk epic, historic commander of the White Horde and founder of the separate Noghay Horde during the last years of the 14th century. In 1407 he raided the Volga Bulgars, and the following year he organized a destructive Tatar invasion of Russia as punishment for its failure to pay tribute for many years. Idegäy burned Nizhni Novgorod, Gorodets, Rostov and several other towns but was unable to take Moscow, though his troops destroyed its suburbs. According to the Tatar folk epic, Idegäy said of his bow:

My bow is resilient and tight,
I'll try to bend my bow.
I have a steel arrow,
It is parti-coloured.
Its tail is crow's feather.

(For the use of firearms among the Volga Bulgars, see below under 'Fortifications & Siege Warfare'.)

Helmets

Judging by manuscript sources such as the miniatures in the Russian *Radzivilovskaya Chronicle*, almost all Volga Bulgar warriors would have worn a helmet. The written evidence of Arab and other Muslim travellers points to the existence of two major forms, though only one has yet been found during archeological excavations. The first was a sphero-conical form of directly-riveted plate construction, with a long tube for a plume and a long protective nasal bar. This is essentially the same structure that is widely found across Russia and Northern, Central and Inner Asia.

Another form of helmet that was used during the 12th and 13th centuries was again of sphero-conical shape but had a rectangular cut-out above the face, which was in turn covered by a face-mask serving as a protective visor. One such visor-mask came to the State Historical Museum of Tatarstan from the local museum in Chistopol. Although its precise find location remains unclear, this origin permits us to say with reasonable certainty that the face-mask visor was highly likely to have been found within the territory of Tatarstan and Volga Bulgaria.

Several very similar mask-visors have been found, together with their associated helmets, in the Middle Dnieper region of Russia and the Ukraine. They are understood to have been used by warriors of the 'Black Klobuki' – a semi-nomadic people of Turkish origin who had migrated to this region on the frontiers between forest and steppe when forced out of the western steppes by more powerful rivals. Such 'Black Klobuki' masks are remarkably realistic; indeed, some scholars have even suggested that they were attempted portraits of their owners. In contrast, the mask from Volga Bulgar territory is simpler and offers a more stylized representation of a face, with wide-set, slightly slanting eyes. The protruding, somewhat rounded nose has two small holes as nostrils, and on the forehead are the reasonably well-preserved remains of a decoration of small dots.

At the upper edge of the face a square steel plate is attached by a large rivet, this being the remains of a device (perhaps hinged) by which the mask was fastened to the missing helmet. Unless there was some other means of securing the face-mask visor, such as a leather strap, one might suppose that there would

Finely crafted archer's silver wrist-bracer; according to N. Federova, this was made in the Khanate of Volga Bulgaria during the 10th to 14th centuries. (Kama Archaeological & Ethnographical Expedition Finds; Perm Museum)

Elements from helmets, found in the territories of the Volga Bulgars: (1) & (2): A long plume-holder tube and a broken nasal.(3): An anthropomorphic steel mask-visor. (A.S. Sheps, after I. Izmailov)

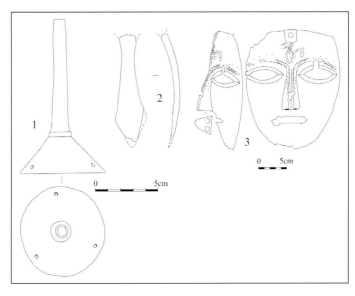

have been a danger of the visor flipping up and exposing the wearer's face in battle. On the other hand, the same single-hinged attachment at the forehead was used in many visored bascinets in 14th- and early 15th-century Europe, especially in Germany, Central Europe and Italy.

A very similar mask, but with a closed mouth, was found during excavations at Serensk in the Kaluga region of western Russia. This has been dated by A. Kirpichnikov to the first half of the 13th century. Much later examples continued to be used in parts of the Caucasus until the early 19th century. Unfortunately, no masked helmets themselves are yet known to have been found within the territory of the Volga Bulgars, though they were certainly used.

Mask-visor found in the territory of the Volga Bulgar Khanate. (Photo via M. Gorelik)

Armour

Assorted evidence from the medieval period shows that the armour worn by the early Volga Bulgars was at a high level of development. Arab writers such as Ibn Rushd, al-Muqaddasi and al-Gardizi all noted that Bulgar warriors had mail hauberks, and their statements have been confirmed by modern archaeology. Taken together, such evidence indicates that mail armour, first recorded in the 8th to 10th centuries, soon became almost standard equipment amongst the Volga Bulgar military elite. Indeed, during the 10th and 11th centuries mail hauberks became the dominant form of body protection, and were used more widely despite the substantial cost of their manufacture. Less is known about leather lamellar armour and shields, though evidence from neighbouring and related cultures strongly suggests that these were widely used.

Late medieval helmet found near the Kama river, of the type used by several peoples near the Ural Mountains. (Historical Museum, Perm; photo Y. Kuleshov)

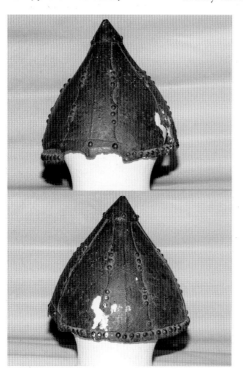

Archaeological research shows that Volga Bulgar mail armour was structurally the same as that used in Russia before the Mongol invasions. Most consisted of relatively short mail shirts rather than full-length hauberks as used in Western Europe, generally around 80cm (31.5in) from neck to hem, and consisting of from 100 to 125 rows of mail rings. The average width was about 90 to 95cm (35.5–37.4in) at the shoulders, reducing to 55 to 60cm (21.7–23.6in) at the waist. The sleeves were similarly short, normally up to 20cm (c.8in) long. The diameter of the individual mail rings varied from 1 to 1.3cm (0.39–0.51in), made from wire between 1 and 2mm (0.04–0.08in) thick. Generally speaking, each mail link was interconnected with four others.

Also found in the territory of the Volga Bulgars were fragments of iron plate armour dating from the 12th to 13th centuries, though the surviving pieces are too fragmentary to permit accurate reconstruction. In one exceptionally rare case a few fragments of leather armour survive, though in very poor condition; all that can be said is that the lamellae of this leather cuirass consisted of thick plates, perhaps of rawhide, and each measuring about 13 x 9cm (5.1 x 3.5 inches). Most comparable fragments are made of metal; their sizes and shapes vary considerably, perhaps indicating that a variety of different types of both lamellar and scale armours were manufactured.

During the 13th century, if not slightly earlier, there was increasing contact between East and West, which might account for the appearance of mail armours with flat rings rather than those made from round-section drawn wire, as well as armours made from small scales and, perhaps, the use of kite-shaped shields, as well as the already mentioned helmets with face-mask visors.

When Volga Bulgaria was incorporated into the territory of the Khanate of Kazan, its warriors started to use the same weapons and armour as those used by the Mongol-Tatars and the Kipchak Turks, probably having imported equipment from these peoples. This included metal chest discs and long lamellar cuirasses, which were worn over thickly quilted or padded kaftan-coats which served as shock-absorbent 'soft armour'.

Shields

The shields used in early medieval Europe were generally round, flat, and about 1m (39in) in diameter. They had a hemispherical boss over a central hole, behind which was quite a long grip bar. Such shields were probably used throughout most of European Russia and even the Volga Bulgar region. Around the same time as the 13th-century Mongol invasions or a little later, a new type of shield began to be adopted in several areas, copied from the Mongols. These were also round, but of essentially a flattened conical shape, with an almost flat, often decoratively-engraved boss. Their basic construction consisted of a spiral of slender cane held together by threads; the latter permitted richly coloured and sometimes elaborate decoration, plus various tassels made of horsehair. In some examples the surface was colourfully painted. The Bulgars used the originally Turkish name of *kalkan* for such shields. Some manuscript illustrations in the Russian *Radzivilovskaya Chronicle* are believed to show Volga Bulgar foot-soldiers using both these round shields and the kite-shaped shields also carried by Russian warriors.

An overview of the general development of Volga Bulgar military equipment from the late 12th or early 13th century onwards suggests much the same picture as could be seen throughout Europe – one of increasing weight and protective capabilities. Just as was the case amongst the opposing Rus' *druzhinas*, the most important of the 'knightly' Volga Bulgar armoured cavalry used sabres, swords, axes (which were sometimes ornamented), spears (with some edged heads to permit a lateral blow), bronze maces (which were sometimes decoratively gilded), war-flails or *kistens* as they were known in Russian, coats of mail, and helmets. The light cavalry had leather armour, broader-leaved spearheads, universal axes, bronze *kistens*, and archery equipment. The evidence shows that, as among neighbouring peoples,

This silver plate found at Muji was, according to N. Federova, made in Volga Bulgar territory; it shows a fully armoured cavalryman (see enlargement on title page). He wears a frame-and-segment helmet with a deep mail aventail; this, and the short sleeves of a mail shirt, are differentiated from the long lamellar (?) cuirass. The claw-shaped item below the belt on his left side may be a bowcase. (Kama Archaeological & Ethnographical Expedition Finds; Perm Museum)

(1) to (14): Iron lamellae from cuirasses dating from the 10th to 13th centuries. (16) to (25): Iron scales from cuirasses dating from the 12th to 14th centuries. (A.S. Sheps, after I. Izmailov)

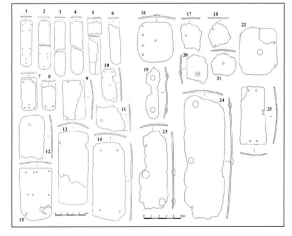

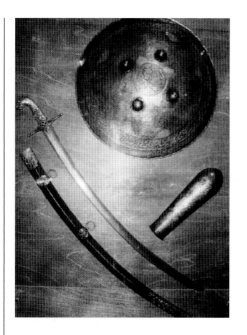

armour was specifically designed to protect against these weapons, since, by and large, the Volga Bulgars did not anticipate having to fight enemies who were very different from themselves.

An interesting fact mentioned by the Muslim traveller al-Garnati was that when on campaign the Volga Bulgars carried their armour in special bags loaded in horse-drawn vehicles, just as Russian warriors did during the same period. On the other hand, the evidence also shows that the armour used by these Volga Bulgars was generally lighter than that of their Russian opponents, and certainly lighter than that of Western Europeans. For example, there is no evidence of them using long-sleeved mail hauberks, mail mittens or chausses. This was because their primary opponents remained the lightly armoured and generally nomadic steppe peoples from further east and south. Nonetheless, one could argue that the Volga Bulgars served as the most distant easternmost outpost of European civilization, facing the world of the nomadic peoples of the steppes.

Kazan Tatar shield, vambrace and sabre dating from the 16th century. (State Historical Museum of Tatarstan, Kazan; photo V. Shpakovsky)

The corner of a reconstructed timber fortified wall of the type used by both Volga Bulgars and Russians. The joints are cut in such a way that the logs cannot be pulled outwards. (Photo V. Shpakovsky)

FORTIFICATIONS & SIEGE WARFARE

The fortifications of the Volga Bulgars were typical for a region that was rich in timber. Thus walls were of relatively simple timber construction, strengthened by towers and fronted by deep moats.[6] However, such fortifications were vulnerable to attack by fire, especially in the dry months of summer, and this vulnerability was dramatically displayed during a siege of Bilyar in the autumn of 1236. This was the climactic battle that decided the fate of the Volga Bulgars' capital city – and, indeed, their state – during the Mongol invasions. Eventually it ended with the total destruction of Bilyar and the grisly massacre of its population, estimated at several tens of thousands of deaths.

According to the historical sources, after the battle of the Samara Bend in which a Volga Bulgar force drove off a Mongol army, the Bulgars renovated and strengthened the entire fortifications of Bilyar. The city was encircled with a third wall, 11km (6.8 miles) long, this time made of both stone and timber, with a deep moat. However, after the Mongols laid siege to the city it was only able to hold out for 45 days. Archaeological excavations uncovered the remains of the burned fortifications and the unburied remains of its slaughtered population scattered all across Bilyar, confirming the evidence of Kazan Tatar legends and of Russian chronicles. In the latter we read that the Mongols 'took the glorious Great City of Bulghar and massacred everybody, from monks to babies, and took many goods and set fire to the city and captured their land'.

One reason why the Mongol invaders showed such ruthless savagery was because one of Ghengis Khan's sons was killed during their storming of the town of Kulkan. In revenge the Mongols tried to wipe Bilyar off the face of the earth; to a great extent they succeeded, and when, some years later, some Bulgars tried to revive their 'Great City' their attempt

6 See MAA 367, *Medieval Russian Armies 1250–1500*

failed. The Mongols then moved on to destroy many other Volga Bulgar towns before turning against the Rus'. However, the north of the country remained intact and attracted many survivors, who resettled territory to the north and west of the old Volga Bulgar heartlands.

Timber and moat fortifications

Recent archaeological excavations, plus the evidence of medieval historical sources, confirm that some Volga Bulgar towns had notably strong wooden fortifications. Although Bilyar was unusual in also possessing some stone towers, its three outermost circuits of defences basically consisted of massive earth ramparts plus two internal fortifications or citadels. In front of the first rampart, which was topped by a substantial timber wall with towers spaced at intervals, was a further 'front wall' called a *tyn* or timber fence. The most commonly used wood for such walls was oak, although sometimes less fire-resistant pine was also used. Stone had similarly been used as a building material for many centuries, though usually only to provide foundations for fortified towers; otherwise the Volga Bulgars normally only used stone construction for their most important buildings, including mosques or palaces. A few other stone towers were seen in the *kremlins* (citadels) of Kazan and the city of Bulgar, yet even in the mid-16th century the walls of Kazan's kremlin were still made of timber, and proved highly vulnerable to Ivan the Terrible's cannon.

Siege machinery

The most widely used tactic amongst the Volga Bulgars themselves was a sudden raid against an enemy town by mobile detachments consisting of small numbers of cavalry, and the same sort of raiding also proved to be effective against Russia during that period. Notably successful examples were the taking of Murom in 1088, and of Ustug in 1218. If these sudden attacks brought no positive results the Bulgars often retreated, which strongly suggests that they did not take significant siege weaponry on such campaigns. On the other hand, there is evidence that they did possess certain types of offensive or defensive siege weapons. The written sources state that they occasionally used large crossbows, as well as stone-throwing machines comparable to the *manjaniqs* employed by their fellow Muslims in Central Asia and the Middle East. These were certainly used in defence of their own towns, for example during the sieges of Bilyar and Kazan.[7]

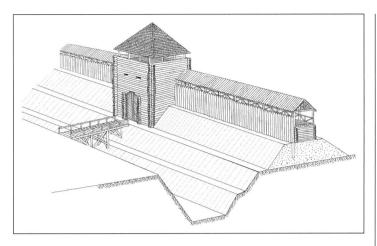

The moat and timber wall of Kazan in the 10th and 11th centuries. Alternative reconstructions of fortifications between the 10th and 14th centuries show the forward slope of the rampart above the moat faced with a criss-cross pattern of tree-trunks or heavy timbers staked down, with grass growing between them. Sharpened stakes were also planted at intervals in wet moats. (A.S. Sheps, after A. Gubidyllin)

The so-called Şaytan Qalası or 'Devil's Tower' at Elabugha was part of a 12th-century Volga Bulgar fortress that combined stone towers with timber walls. (Photo V. Shpakovsky)

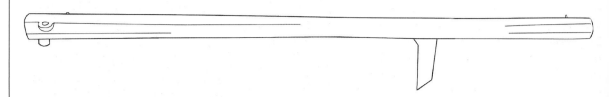

The barrel of a 16th-century 'hook-gun' or harquebus, known in Russian as a *zatinnaya pishal* or *gakovnitsa.* This example has a barrel nearly 4ft 6in long, of 0.9in calibre. (A.S. Sheps, after I. Ismailov)

Firearms

Hand-held firearms became known in Eastern Europe at quite an early date. In Russia their first recorded use was at the end of the 14th century, but by that time the citizens of the Volga Bulgar Khanate are already understood to have possessed some sort of firearms. For example, when the Grand Prince Dmitrii Ivanovich 'Donskoy' of Muscovy sent a large army against the Bulgars in 1376, the defenders reportedly used firearms. According to the chronicler's account of this campaign, the defenders of Bulgar came out of their fortifications 'and began fighting and shooting, and some of them made thunder standing at the walls, frightening the Russian forces'.

On the other hand, such 'thunder' weapons may not yet have been bullet-shooting guns or cannon, and may perhaps have been comparable to the arrow- or bolt-shooting cannon used in the Mamluk Sultanate of Egypt and Syria. A remarkably well-made all-iron arrow was in fact found in the ruined fortifications of the Russian city of Vladimir. It is almost 2m (6.6ft) long, and had three flights wrought or beaten from the thickened rear part of its shaft. Supposedly dating from the 13th or more likely the 14th century, such a sophisticated and terrifying weapon is unlikely to have been used by the Russians, and was more probably shot or fired at Vladimir during one of the Tatar-Mongol sieges of the city.

The design of the first gunpowder weapons in this region was undeniably simple. They consisted of forged or cast pipes sealed at one end and attached to a primitive wooden bedding. Nevertheless their dimensions varied greatly, including heavy barrels that had to be placed on a substantial stand, but also others that could be held by one man in his hands.

During the last quarter of the 15th century, the so-called *zatinnaya pishal* appeared. Its name indicated that it was normally positioned behind a wooden palisade. It was also known by the name *gakovnitsa,* because the barrel incorporated a hook (*gak*) that when placed over a barricade absorbed the recoil of the gun when fired – a design feature widely seen in the West. The barrel of one such early 'hook-gun' is now on show in the Tatarstan State Historical Museum; the forged barrel is octagonal in section, 135cm (53.2in) long, with a calibre of 23mm (0.9in), and of rather coarse workmanship. This gun is thought to date from the second half of the 16th century, but may even have been one of the weapons that were used by both sides during the final siege of Kazan in 1552.

This leaves one interesting question unanswered. If the Volga Bulgars first used some sort of gunpowder weapon against the Russians in 1376, and again six years later against Khan Toqtamysh of the Golden Horde in 1382, were these weapons introduced from the West or from the East – from Europe, or from China via the Mongol states?

CONCLUSIONS

The history of warfare amongst the Volga Bulgars illustrates the interesting phenomenon of how a relatively small society, under military threat from several stronger neighbours, adopted differing military cultures and technologies. During the long period of its pre-Mongol history the Volga Bulgar Khanate possessed a military arsenal that had evolved under strong influence from the Rus'. As a result the elite cavalry were fully armoured, almost like Western knights, but also made use of various examples of steppe nomad equipment. They carried Western swords as well as Eastern sabres; they sometimes rode using spurs, which were barely known amongst the nomads; and their spears had sharp edges as well as thrusting points. They protected themselves with early forms of round shield with a pronounced boss, and also soon adopted the kite-shaped shield, while also wearing both mail and lamellar or scale armour. Seen from a distance, they would not have appeared so very dissimilar from the Norman knights in the Bayeux Tapestry.

During the Mongol/Tatar occupation, however, the various peoples of the Volga Bulgar region were largely assimilated into Mongol society (at least militarily), and adopted their conquerors' military culture and tactics. Nevertheless, being a highly developed region with many towns and cities, the new, post-conquest Volga Bulgaria became a separate khanate in its own right, and could field urban militias that fought on foot. These were very similar to those of Russian towns who were similarly under Mongol rule or suzerainty. The troops involved used forms of weapon that were uncommon amongst the military cultures of Eurasian steppe peoples, who, like the dominant Tatars, relied upon horse-archery. Included in this context were the crossbows, cannon, and hand-held harquebus guns that the people of Volga Bulgaria and the Khanate of Kazan used in their struggles against the Russians. Much the same was true of their military architecture, with formidable citadels being just as much a feature of the Khanate of Kazan as they were amongst the Rus' of Muscovy. Most notable of all, the first known use of firearms in the easternmost parts of Europe took place in 1376 in the territory of Volga Bulgaria rather than in the Principality of Moscow.

The excavated ruins of late medieval Kazan are displayed beneath a glass cover in the modern city. (Photo V. Shpakovsky)

Bronze belt buckle from Kazan, 10th–11th centuries. (ex-Valeev & Valeeva-Suleimanova)

FURTHER READING

Bakhshi, I. (ed.), *Dzhafar Tarikhi, Vol. 1. Svod Bulgarskikh Letpisei 1680 g* (Orenburg & Kazan, 1993). This is a Russian translation of the 13th-century *Gazi Baraj Karikhi*, preserved in a 17th-century Bulgar Turkic chronicle, confiscated but also translated by the NKVD Soviet political police in 1939.

Baladhuri, Ahmad al- (tr. P.K. Hitti & F.C. Murgotten), *The Origins of the Islamic State* (London; Vol 1, 1916; Vol. 2, 1924)

Balkhi, Abu Zaid Ahmad Ibn Sahl al- (tr. C. Huart), *Ashkal Al-Belad. Le livre de la Creation et de l'histoire d'Abou-Zeid, Ahmed ben Sahl al-Balkhi publie et traduit d'apres de manuscrit de Constantinople* (Paris, 1899–1919)

Chalicova, E.A., & Chalikov, A.H, 'Altungam an der Kama und in Ural (Das Graberfeld von Bolschie Tigani)', in *Regeszeti Fuzeter*, ser. 2, 21 (Budapest, 1981)

Gorelik, M.V., 'Oriental Armour of the Near and Middle East from the Fifteenth Century as shown in Works of Art', in R. Elgood (ed.), *Islamic Arms and Armour* (London, 1979)

Gorelik, M.V., 'Mongolo-Tatarskoe Zashitnoe Vooryzhenie Vtoroy Polovini XIV – nachala XV vv.' ('Mongol-Tatar Defensive Armament - second half of the 14th to the early 15th centuries'), in (anon. ed.) *Kulikovskaya Bitva v Istorii I Kulture Nashey Rodini* (The Battle of Kulikovo in the History and Culture of our Motherland) (Moscow, 1983)

Gubaydullin, A.M., *Fortifikatsia gorodish Volzhskoy Bulgarii* (Fortification of the Volga Bulgaria Settlements) (Kazan, 2002)

Ibn Fadlan, Ahmad (tr. M. Canard), *Voyage chez les Bulgares de la Volga* (Paris, 1988)

Ibn-Rustah, Ahmad al-Isfahani (Abu Ali Ahmad Ibn Umar) (ed. M.J. De Goeje), *Kitab al-A'lak al-Nafisa* (Book of Precious Records) (Leiden, 1892)

Istakhri, Abu Ishaq Ibrahim al-Farisi al- (ed. W. Ouseley), *The Oriental Geography of Ebn Haukal, an Arabian traveller of the Tenth Century* (London, 1800). NB: this work was wrongly attributed to Ibn Hawqal.

Izmailov, I.L., Zashchitniki 'Stenui Iskandera' - *Vooruzhenue, voennoe iskussmvo i voennaya ismoruya Volgasskoi Bulgarii X-XIII vv* (Defenders of 'Alexander's Wall'. Armament, military arts and military systems of the Volga Bulgars 10th–13th centuries) (Kazan, 2008)

Izmailov, I.L. (et al, eds.), *Volgskaya Bulgariya in Mongolskoe Nashchestvie* (Volga Bulgars and the Mongol Invasion) (Kazan, 1988)

Izmailov, I.L., *Vooryzhenie i Voennoe Delo Naselenia Volzhskoy Bulgarii X-nachala XIII vv.* (Weaponry and Military Affairs of the Volga Bulgarian Population, 10th–early 13th centuries) (Magadan–Kazan, 1997)

Kuchkin, V.A., 'O marshrytah poxodov drevnerusskih knyazey na gosudarstvo voljskih bulgar v XII- pervoy treti XIII v.' ('The ways of ancient Russian princely campaigns against the Volga Bulgar state, 12th - first third of 13th century'), in V.A. Kuchkin (ed.), *Volgo-Okskoe Mezhdurech'e i Nizhniy Novgorod v Srednie Veka* (Volga-Oka confluence and Nizhniy Novgorod in the Medieval Centuries) (Nizhniy Novgorod, 2011)

Makovskaya, L.N., *Ruchnoye Ognestrelnoe Oryzhye Russkoy Armee Kontsa XIV–XVIII vv* (Hand-held Firearms of the Russian Army from the end of the 14th to the 18th Century) (Moscow, 1992)

Mas'udi, al- (ed. & tr. C. Barbier de Maynard & P. de Coutieille),
 Les Prairies d'Or. Muruj al-Dhahab (Paris, 1861–64)

Mazhitov, N.A., *Kurgani Yuzhnogo Urala VIII-XII vv* (Grave Sites of
 the Southern Urals 8th–12th centuries) (Moscow, 1981)

Murkasuim, U., & Rafael, Kh. (eds.), *Istoriya Tatar s Drevneishikh Vremen
 v Semi Tomakh, Volume 3, Ulus Dzhuchi (Zolotaya Orda) XIII-seredina
 XV v.* (Kazan, 2009)

Penskoy, V.V., 'Ot "neznaushih boevogo poryadka" sklavov i antov k
 "stene" Sveatoslava' ('From "inexperienced in military tactics"
 Sklavy and Anty to the "battle wall" of Sveatoslav'), in *The History
 in Details*, 3 (2012)

Pletnyeva, S.A., *Kochevniki Srednevekoviy* (Nomads of the Middle Ages)
 (Moscow, 1982)

Pletnyeva, S.A., *Stepi Eurasii b Epokhu Srednevekoyva* (Moscow, 1981)

Pritsak, O., 'The Proto-Bulgarian military inventory inscriptions', in
 Studia Turco-Hungarica, 5 (Budapest, 1981)

Sedov, V.V., *Finno-Ugri in Balti v Epokhu Srednevekovya* (Finno-Ugrians
 and Balts in the Middle Ages (Moscow, 1987)

Seleznev, F.A., 'Liubov' k detyam kak dvigatel' istorii: Jurii Dolgoruky
 i russko-bulgarskie otnosheniya v pervoy polovine XII v.' ('The
 love of children as the engine of history: Jurii Dolgoruky and
 Russian-Bulgar relations in the first half of the 12th century'), in
 The History in Details, 3 (2012)

Shirokorad, A.B., *Russkie piraty* (Russian pirates) (Moscow, 2007)

Smirnov, A.P., *Volzhskie bulgary* (Volga Bulgars) (Moscow, 1951)

Valeev, F.K., & Valeeva-Suleimanova, G.F., *Drevnee Iskusstvo Tatarstana*
 (Early History of Tatarstan) (Kazan, 2002)

Yaqut al-Hamawi (ed. H.F. Wüstenfeld), *Jacut's Geographisches Wörterbuch
 [Kitab Mujam al-Buldan]* (Leipzig, 1866)

PLATE COMMENTARIES

A: BULGARS & SUBJECTS, 9th–10th CENTURIES

A1: Bulgar leader, 10th century

Supervising the building of a fortress in the eastern part of the khanate, this high-ranking individual already shows the influence of the Islamic world in the patterned covering of his fur-lined, sleeveless coat and split-brim hat, the fabrics being imported from Iraq or Iran. In other respects his clothing and military equipment remain typical of the western Eurasian steppes and of the Khazar Khanate from which the Volga Bulgars emerged. A short, short-sleeved mail hauberk is worn beneath his coat and over a shirt, and baggy trousers are tucked into soft-leather riding boots. A straight, narrow-bladed sword with an angled hilt, and a dagger, are suspended from a belt with gilt bronze attachment points, stiffeners and pendant straps. By this period the arms and armour, and even to some extent the costume, of the ruling and military elites of the eastern and central Islamic lands were themselves under growing Turkish Central Asian influence.

A2: Bulgar cavalryman, 9th–10th centuries

This warrior again highlights the shared military-technological traditions of the Eurasian steppes, the Byzantine Empire and much of the Islamic world during the early medieval period. This is particularly apparent in the helmet that he holds; of segmented iron construction, it has a large brow-and-eye plate and a nasal bar, and an attached mail aventail covering the face. Over his mail shirt he wears a shorter lamellar iron

cuirass; its plates cover only the front and sides, and it is secured at the rear by a waist strap and crossed shoulder straps. The sword illustrates a growing preference for slightly curved, single-edged swords, which were in the process of evolving into the fully formed sabre. The belt has several pendant straps, some of which were used to carry archery equipment when required; this style was also spreading from the steppe cultures to the eastern and central provinces of the Islamic world. Other typical weapons would be a long spear with a flattened diamond-section blade, and a short-hafted axe with a hammerhead extension above the socket. The bridle and the breast and crupper straps securing the leather-covered wooden saddle are decorated with bronze studs and animal-tail tassels; the iron bit has long *psalion*-bars, a feature that would not become widely used in the Islamic world.

A3: Infantry archer of subject tribe, 10th century

Though the Volga Bulgars were of Turkic steppe origins, and are now believed to have taken over from a pre-existing Turkic elite, much of their new territory was still inhabited by peoples of Finnish or Ugrian origin. The military traditions of these peoples differed from those of their Turkic rulers, and are here represented by an unarmoured foot-soldier wearing a fur-lined woollen coat over an off-white linen shirt, and trousers tied at the ankle over leather shoes. His primary weapon is a massive recurved bow, bound with birch-bark and with bone plates at the grip – part of a military-technological heritage that the Finns shared with most of their Slav neighbours. Note the leather quiver with a bronze ornament, holding arrowheads uppermost. His other arms are a substantial axe, which was as much a working tool as a weapon, and a simple dagger which could also serve more peaceful purposes.

B: BULGARS & ALLIES, 11th–12th CENTURIES

B1: Bulgar cavalryman, 11th–12th centuries

This warrior is leading a sortie from the gatehouse and over the moat bridge of a substantial timber fortress. By the 11th century there were increasing similarities between the military equipment used by the Volga Bulgar Khanate and its Russian rivals. This is demonstrated by the scale cuirass worn over his mail shirt, and by his single-piece iron helmet which has a gilded plume-holder, ornate brow plate, rim-band, and large, curved nasal; note too the extended, leather-edged aventail. Influences flowed in both directions, however; the archery equipment typical of the Turkic Volga Bulgars – here a bowcase buckled to hang above the sword, and a quiver on the right hip – was also used in Russian armies. To a lesser extent this was similarly true of the slightly curved proto-sabre (which our man has broken, and dropped), the decorated battleaxe that he wields instead, and his horse-harness.

B2: Khanty tribal warrior, 11th–12th centuries

Although the Khanty were a forest-dwelling Finnish tribal people, their military culture was substantially influenced by the Turco-Mongol peoples of the steppes. Nevertheless they retained certain distinctive features (perhaps most notably, barbed spearheads). This archer wears a bulky, possibly fur-lined long-sleeved tunic, with a substantial hood thrown back from the shoulders over his lamellar iron cuirass, which protects both front and back of the torso; the overlapping curved plates to protect the outside of his arms are a reconstruction based on iconographic sources. The quiver is of a simple, vertically hung type suitable for archery on foot, and his wrist-mounted combination bracer and arrow-guide is of a type that could be seen as far east as China. Note the

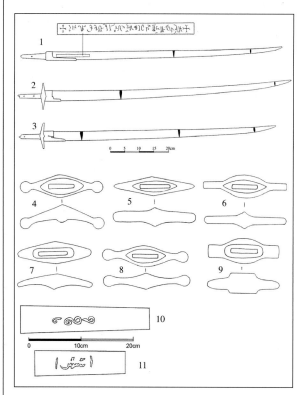

(1) to (3): Volga Bulgar sabres of the 10th and 11th centuries. (4) to (9): Vertical and side views of various types of sabre hilts. (10) & (11): Decoration and inscription on sabre blades from Volga Bulgar territory. (A.S. Sheps, after I. Ismailov)

distinctive ring pommel of his sword, made by bending the iron tang into a circle, and its angled 'hatchet' tip, a feature shared with Siberian peoples.

B3: Mari tribal warrior, 11th century
The Mari were another Finnish tribal people who sometimes acknowledged Volga Bulgar suzerainty. They appear to have been under stronger Slavic or Western military influence; this man's simple domed helmet has an iron frame filled in with hardened leather segments, and his straight sword blade was probably made in the Rhineland, although its bronze hilt may have been added in Russia.

C: THE MONGOL CONQUEST, MID-13th CENTURY

C1: Bulgar *amir*
This aristocratic leader is kicking free from his dying horse to make a last stand in a Muslim cemetery. By the 12th and 13th centuries, Volga Bulgar warriors were characterized by a number of distinctive forms of equipment; most of these reflected traditions originating in the previous Khazar Khanate of the western steppes, while others were shared with Turkic peoples of that region. They included the very finely made one-piece iron helmet with an anthropomorphic face-mask visor, and the war-flail. The flail shown here has a bronze head attached to the haft by rawhide thongs; this peculiar cavalry weapon would enter the mythology of Central and Western Europe as a weapon of demons and other evil aliens. The iron cuirass, three rows shorter at the back than the front, has an embossed dome centred on each scale; just visible at the chest is a larger plate bearing a Turkish tribal *tagma*. The mail hauberk worn beneath the cuirass reaches to just below the elbows and above the knees; note too the rather rudimentary iron vambraces and gauntlets.

C2: Mordvin nobleman
Archaeological evidence shows that the Mordvin (Mordovian) people, who inhabited territory south-west of the heartland of the Volga Bulgar Khanate, used mixed military equipment of Western and probably Turco-Mongol steppe origin; consequently, straight, double-edged swords of Russian or European origin were wielded by warriors whose lamellar armour was identical to that of the Volga Bulgars. Under his lamellar cuirass the decoration on this fighting man's tunic is specifically Mordvin, though embroidered rectangles above the elbows might recall the more elaborate *tiraz* fabrics which were used as marks of elite status and loyalty in the Islamic Caliphate. His iron helmet has a reinforcement band partway around the rim, and 'eyebrow' reinforcement associated with the nasal bar.

C3: Mongol warrior
The conquering Mongols would add several new features to the military technology of the Volga Bulgars; much of it already showed Chinese influence, as seen in this figure of a wounded cavalryman. His fallen helmet is of complex segmented and framed construction with a frontal brim (in its absence, note his hairstyle, with shaven scalp and looped side-plaits.) The arm-flaps and body of his long cuirass have iron scales under the yellow fabric covering, each secured by two gilded rivets at its upper left corner. The scales do not extend over the upper chest, where a red 'cloud' motif is just visible under the cape-like shoulder defence, which itself seems to be of fabric-covered leather without iron scales. Under his armour he wears a long woollen coat with a deeply overlapping double-breasted front. His shield is of spiral-cane construction, held together and decorated by coloured cotton threads; it has an iron boss and cross-shaped iron reinforcements.

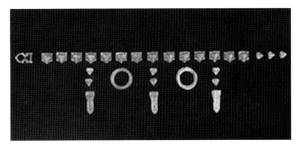

Medieval warrior's belt ornaments found in Mordovian territory. (Mordovian Republic United Museum of Regional Studies, Saransk, Russian Federation)

D: VOLGA BULGARIAN KHANATE UNDER THE MONGOLS, 14th CENTURY

D1: Volga Bulgar nobleman
It appears that like many other recently conquered peoples, the surviving aristocracy of the Volga Bulgar Khanate rapidly adopted many aspects of Mongol costume as a means of demonstrating allegiance to their new overlords. This is shown here by the nobleman's quilted, semi-rigid hat; the looped plaits of his hairstyle; and the Chinese silk coat, flared out in pleats from a line around the hips. The system of leather straps and garters (here in red) which hold up his boots seems to have been very characteristic of the western Mongol khanates and their vassals in what is now south-western Russia. His sword, though straight and double-edged, is in the Chinese rather than the Western European tradition of such weapons.

D2: Ugrian warrior
The Ugrian peoples of north-western Siberia strongly resisted both Mongol and subsequently Russian conquest. Their military equipment was in many respects old-fashioned, while also reflecting the influences of both East and West. The combined eye-piece and nasal on this domed helmet is thought to have been distinctively Ugrian, though the short-sleeved mail hauberk with a long, slit hem would have been imported or captured from elsewhere. Though not shown here, an interesting feature of such warriors' gear seems to have been domed iron protectors apparently riveted to soft-leather bands worn around the elbows and knees. Though they are hidden at this angle, he would have a bowcase and a long, slightly curved, angle-hilted sabre suspended from the left side of his belt.

D3: Mongol warrior of the Golden Horde, early 14th century
In contrast to the fairly primitive equipment of the Ugrian warrior, this elite cavalryman from the Golden Horde illustrates the sophistication of the Volga Bulgar Khanate's western Mongol overlords. His tall, pointed, one-piece steel helmet, here with a woollen tuft around the plume-holder, is in a style that would remain popular in Russia for centuries. Here the only body protection is a mail hauberk, though in battle he is likely to have added a lamellar or a scale-lined armour. The stiffness of his short-sleeved coat probably reflects the abundant use of silk plus a thick lining rather than any protective function. He wears two belts – one for a bowcase and a box-quiver, and one for his sword – over his mail hauberk, quilted undercoat, and deeply overlapped kaftan-coat of 'cloud-pattern' silk; the latter is slit from the hem to the hip at both sides.

(1) & (2) Bronze strap-end from a belt, and buckle plate, 13th century (Bulgar National Historical-Architectural Museum); (3) bronze buckle plate, 13th or early 14th century, from the Astrakhan governorate (Hermitage Museum, St Petersburg); (4) bronze Bulgar buckle plate from Vtorara Polovina, 13th century (State Historical Museum of Tatarstan, Kazan); (5) bronze Bulgar buckle plate from Vtorara Polovina, 13th or early 14th century. (Bulgar National Historical-Architectural Museum; ex-Murkasuim & Rafael, see 'Further Reading')

E: THE *USHKUYNIKI* MENACE, 14th–15th CENTURIES

E1: High-status Bulgar warrior, 14th–15th centuries

In this period there were considerable similarities between the armed forces of the Volga Bulgars and of the Russian frontier principalities which were steadily encroaching upon their territory; both peoples were initially under Mongol suzerainty, though this was steadily weakening in Russia. The segmented helmet, with its very deep rim-band and nasal and extensive mail aventail, is nevertheless more typical of the Turco-Mongol peoples of the steppes and Middle East. Perhaps because his unit is operating in dense forest to watch the activities of Russian river-pirates, this warrior otherwise relies only upon an iron lamellar cuirass over a thickly quilted 'soft armour' coat; note the leather extension below the lames at the front, and the coloured sash. The wearing of shoes and short 'puttees', rather than leather boots, would also suggest that he does not expect to ride very far. The elaborately-painted shield is of Mongol type, of spiral-cane construction covered with leather or parchment.

E2: Archer, 14th–15th centuries

This Volga Bulgar foot-soldier wears gear practically identical to his Russian *ushkuyniki* foes. The spired steel helmet has an aventail divided at both sides, covering his neck back and front but not the shoulders. The mail hauberk is short-hemmed but has sleeves to below the elbow. Note that the long-sleeved, quilted coat-armour is much shorter at the back than at the front, where it is divided from hem to belly. The slung shield and the archery equipment also resemble Russian styles, though the signalling whistle attached below his arrowhead may have been confined to the Mongols and their Volga Bulgar vassals.

E3: Siberian tribal mercenary, 14th century

Whether many western Siberian warriors fought as mercenaries outside their own homelands east of the Ural Mountains is unclear, but the evidence suggests that their military technology not only remained quite primitive but made use of pieces of equipment originating far from Siberia. In this case the warrior has been given a rather old and battered double-domed, segmented helmet of ultimately Inner Asian, Chinese, or even Tibetan origin, while his axe may have originated far to the west. Three metal discs, perhaps bearing totemic designs, are fixed to the front of the mail hauberk that he wears over a bulky coat of reversed bearskin. The birch-bark shoulder-quiver and bark-wrapped composite bow are indigenous Siberian items, and would seem to be suited to fighting or hunting in forests rather than on the open steppes. Note his hair worn in two plaits from behind the ears.

F: KHANATE OF KAZAN, 15th–EARLY 16th CENTURIES

F1: Khan, early 16th century

The Khanate of Kazan, which inherited the territory and to a large extent the armies of the preceding Khanate of Volga Bulgaria, could field some of the most advanced forces in the post-Mongol world. Its rulers also based their forms of government and their authority upon the Mongol heritage, as was shown in their ceremonial attire (note the hairstyle with two looped plaits on each side). The gold crown worn by the ruling khan in this reconstruction is a hypothetical, simplified version of a surviving Kazan crown of a century or so later. Equally a sign of status is the richly embroidered Chinese silk fabric that covers his typically Mongol double-breasted coat, which flares out in pleats below the hips; it is worn over a loose, very long-sleeved silk robe. His sword-belt, from which the sabre scabbard is suspended on the left and an elaborate purse on the right, would be as richly decorated as his horse-harness. This has lavish gilded ornaments, and the pommel and cantle boards of the saddle are covered with decorated silver plates.

F2: Palace guardsman, late 15th century

Again, this elite cavalryman's military equipment shows continuing strong Mongol influence, especially in his somewhat old-fashioned, long-skirted lamellar cuirass with additional flap-like lamellar upper arm defences. In contrast, the steel vambraces protecting his forearms and the backs of his hands, and greaves protecting his lower legs, are more up to date. The segmented iron helmet, with a frontal brim, has an animal tail or strip of fur tied to the top spike. Very heavy and all-encompassing mail horse-armour would be more common in Iran and Turkey than in the steppe states further north; its presence here, being used by a ruler's guard, might be more symbolic than genuinely military.

F3: Siberian tribal ally, 15th–16th centuries

The establishment of Mongol khanates in western Siberia from the late 13th century onwards had a significant impact upon the military technologies of these and neighbouring regions. As they were increasingly drawn into the mainstream of Central and Inner Asian affairs their warriors had ever greater access to more sophisticated arms, armour and perhaps even horse-harness. Despite rivalries, there was an obvious community of interest between Islamic khanates immediately east of the Ural Mountains and that of Muslim Kazan lying just west of the Urals. The sophistication of this warrior's mail-and-plate cuirass might indicate that it was imported from further afield: from Kazan, Transoxiana, the Middle East, or perhaps even from Russia, where such armours would become very popular. The horizontal rows of lames are linked by mail rings, and plate shoulder defences are riveted to the mail; over the mail sleeves iron vambraces extend upwards to cup the elbows. Iron poleyns protect the knees, with rows of single long lames above and triple short lames below. The aventail of the segmented helmet is of scale-lined fabric, and protects the sides of the face only. As always, the quiver would be balanced on the left hip by a sabre and a case for the short but very powerful composite bow.

G: KHANATE OF KAZAN INFANTRY, 15th– EARLY 16th CENTURIES

G1: Hand-gunner, early 16th century

Firearms were used in the khanate at a remarkably early date, apparently before they appeared in neighbouring Russia. The limited evidence suggests that they were very similar to those used in Central Europe, but it remains unknown whether this new technology reached Kazan from Europe, from the Islamic Middle East, or even from China. In keeping with this uncertainty, we have chosen to reconstruct the weapon whose effects this gunner is showing off after the type used in 15th-century Italy, while his powder horn and bullet pouch are based upon several found in late 15th-century Syria. Meanwhile his costume demonstrates the cultural similarity between the Khanate of Kazan and eastern Russia during this period.

G2: Infantry archer, late 15th century

Despite the new gunpowder technology, composite bows remained the most important and widely used distance weapon in the khanate. Apart from this man's somewhat Russian-looking fur-lined hat, his costume and military equipment bring to mind those used in the fellow-Muslim and fellow-Turkish Ottoman Empire. It is unknown whether such military influence was direct, or arrived via the Principality of Moscow, where Ottoman fashions would soon have a profound impact upon the organization of elite infantry formations.

G3: Fully armoured soldier, late 15th century

While his arms, armour and costume look very different from those of the infantry archer, he nevertheless reflects the influences of Islamic states to the south of the Khanate of Kazan. The mail-and-plate technology used in his helmet as well as his armour may have been developed in eastern Anatolia and western Iran. It was certainly adopted with enthusiasm by the Ottoman Turks, from whose territory this cuirass may actually have been imported. The fringed shoulder plates are directly attached to the mail along their inner edges. The multiple chest plates are linked together by rows of mail; their weight is supported by shoulder straps, and the central disc is edged with fringing. Long vambraces are strapped to the lower arms, over the three-quarter mail sleeves and the coat worn beneath the cuirass. The broad, heavy-bladed sabre also recalls Ottoman weapons.

H: THE FALL OF KAZAN, 1552

H1: Dismounted officer

By the time of the fall of Kazan to Muscovy, Ottoman military influence had increased still further within the forces of the Khanate; the Ottoman Turks already seemed about to take control of the neighbouring steppe regions north of the Black Sea, although in the event Muscovy would triumph in both areas. This officer has dismounted to examine the shocking evidence of Ivan the Terrible's use of heavy bombards firing massive stone balls, and has temporarily handed his gilded mace of command to H3. His distinctive helmet consists of mail and a single 'crown-plate' worn over a substantial arming cap or small turban. His mail cuirass, fastened at the upper

Mail shirt with collar stiffened by leather thongs, 15th–17th centuries. (State Historical Museum of Tatarstan, Kazan; photo V. Shpakovsky)

chest by buckled straps, incorporates only a limited number of plate lames at the front and sides; these, like the mail-linked plate vambraces, are richly decorated with floral motifs and Arabic script. Under the padded coat covered with embroidered silk can be seen leg defences, with plate lames above and mail flaps below the plate poleyns at the knee. All these elements, like his decorated boots and heavy sabre, are now fully within the Turco-Ottoman military tradition.

H2: Noghay warrior

Other Islamic peoples of the western steppes, who would themselves soon be under Muscovite pressure, remained technologically more distinctive – largely because they were still nomadic societies, among whom Mongol military traditions remained strong. Nevertheless, under his distinctive, thickly-quilted coat with hand-protecting sleeve extensions this warrior from the Noghay Khanate north of the Caspian Sea is protected by a mail hauberk, which might incorporate unseen chest and abdomen plates. His tall, thickly-padded hat may also have a rudimentary protective function. He has laid aside his long composite bow, which might typically be painted and have bone plates beneath a leather-bound grip; its scale would resemble that carried by Plate A3. Noticeably long arrows are carried in a decorated leather quiver suspended from his belt at the back; his only other weapon is a simple straight dagger, but a plain leather shield of hardened leather is slung from a guige.

H3: Allied officer, Khanate of Sibir

This cavalryman from Kazan's neighbour immediately east of the Ural Mountains wears an engraved and partially gilded helmet with a very up-to-date sliding nasal bar, mirroring those of the contemporary Islamic Middle East and Balkans. However, his scale-lined, textile-covered cuirass, with its separate shoulder pieces and almost separate sleeves, is within a venerable Sino-Mongol tradition – compare with Plate C3. The exposed steel lamellae of his armoured skirt are remarkably old-fashioned, being structurally similar to armours used in the early medieval Islamic and Byzantine regions. The tip of his sabre and scabbard would be 'hatchet-pointed' in the Siberian style, as on Plate B2. He might carry a spiral-cane shield, with an iron boss and about a dozen coloured tassels spaced around the rim.

INDEX

References to illustrations are shown in **bold**.
References to plates are shown in **bold** with
captions in brackets.